Masters
of cinema

Orson
Welles

2

Contents

Orson Welles in the 1930s.

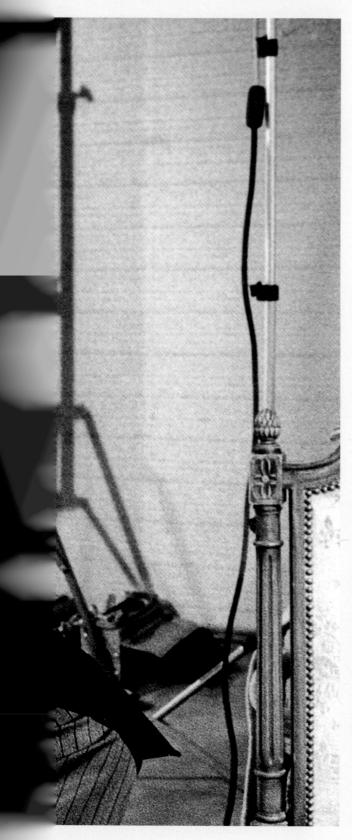

Introduction

The debt that the history of the cinema owes to Orson Welles is more than a matter of the irresistible influence and heartrending passion his films have engendered ('I belong to a generation of directors who decided to make films after seeing *Citizen Kane*', declared François Truffaut, speaking for all his peers). His legacy also, and perhaps primarily, represents a rigorous, enduring example of an artist who possessed the ability to tackle any medium, who fought (not always successfully) the temptations of success and power, and who maintained very clear ideas about the role of the intellectual.

However, Welles's very stature as an artist often tends to impede a true appreciation of his value. What can we say about a director as 'formidable' as Welles, a man who has often been described, sometimes with good reason and sometimes mistakenly, as 'self-destructive' and 'doomed to failure'? How do we approach a body of work that comprises only twelve completed films in a career spanning more than thirty years, especially when at least two of these films were 'officially' ruined by production companies (*The Magnificent Ambersons* and *Touch of Evil*)?

Yet Welles himself helped to blur the issue, particularly given his desire to begin and end his career with two films that were similar in subject and almost identical in narrative structure, projects that gave space to more voices, confronted different ideas and hypotheses and employed sometimes antithetical trajectories. Projects such as these tend to confirm that there is no such thing as a single truth, a single interpretation, a single method, and that what does not hold true for his films cannot be held true for his career. Even so, it is not impossible to juxtapose the life and work of Welles, or to analyse them, but as we proceed we should be aware that ambiguity and contradiction will be our constant companions.

Orson Welles in the 1970s.

Beginnings

Theatre, radio and cinema

Orson Welles in the 1920s.

Right: William Shakespeare's
Twelfth Night by Orson Welles (1932).

The birth of a legend

If we believe the legend — which Welles himself never attempted to refute and indeed substantiated — his exceptional artistic talents became apparent at a very early age. George Orson Welles, born in Kenosha, Wisconsin, on 6 May 1915, was the son of Beatrice Ives, a concert pianist and suffragette, and Richard Head Welles, a part-time inventor from a wealthy Virginia family. The boy was only two years old when he asked his mother to read to him from an original Shakespeare play rather than the children's version. We know that he made his acting début in a production of *Samson and Delilah* at the Chicago Opera in 1918, and that two years later he dressed up as a rabbit in a publicity stunt for the Marshall Field's department store. At the age of ten, he adapted, directed and acted in *Dr Jekyll and Mr Hyde* at the Camp Indianola boys club, and also appeared in a Dickens adaptation, *Scrooge*, at Washington Grade School in Madison, Wisconsin. It is therefore entirely plausible that, in 1925, the *Madison Journal* celebrated the child prodigy's many activities in an article titled 'Cartoonist, Actor, Poet and Only 10'.

By autumn 1926, when Welles entered the Todd School for Boys in Woodstock, Illinois, the theatre had become much more than a simple pastime: he devoted himself to every aspect of the medium, from adapting to producing, from acting to scriptwriting. So great was his enthusiasm that after graduating he departed for Ireland, where he found work as an actor at Dublin's Gate Theatre and later at the Abbey Theatre. He was also allowed to direct at least four plays.

When Welles returned to the United States in 1933, he was fully aware of his abilities as a performer but was nevertheless reluctant to restrict himself to 'being an actor'. Moreover, he had already begun to display symptoms of the 'artistic bulimia' — the compulsion to grapple with several projects at once rather than pursue a single goal — that would afflict him for the rest of his life. Although hired by the actress Katharine Cornell's repertory company for a thirty-six-week tour, he still harboured the ambition to stage his own plays, and he accepted his first radio assignment (for CBS, adapting historical and literary works in serial form for *The American School of the Air*), and collaborated with Roger Hill on an edition of three Shakespeare plays (*Everybody's Shakespeare*), writing revised versions and introductory essays and providing the original illustrations. Finally, he had his first brush with moviemaking, directing an eight-minute short film called *The Hearts of Age*.

The Hearts of Age

Shot in 16mm in June 1934, the film was co-directed by William Vance,[1] who also appeared in it alongside Welles, Virginia Nicholson (who became Welles's first wife in November 1934), Paul Edgerton and Charles O'Neal. The film defies easy analysis, given its elusive narrative framework and meanings. The cavorting of several characters heavily made-up as elderly folk is interspersed with shots of bells, gravestones and a piano keyboard, not to mention the Christmas tree ball caressed and shaken by a white-clad figure. Only Welles himself, playing a character that possibly represents death, could explain the precise meaning of these images (but, of course, he never did). However, this short work is still striking for its highly explicit references to avant-garde European cinema. Some scenes are shot in negative, as in F. W. Murnau's *Nosferatu* (1922), and the characters' make-up is very similar to that used in Robert Wiene's *The Cabinet of Dr. Caligari* (1920).[2] Such references indicate the extent to which the young Welles had already immersed himself in film culture, and also contradict the myth that the young novice director, arriving in Hollywood with no knowledge of film technique, created a masterpiece through a combination of 'ignorance' and 'innocence'.

Theatre and radio

Over the next five years, Welles virtually ignored the cinema and devoted more and more of his time to theatre and radio. His first major opportunity came at the beginning of 1936, when producer John Houseman recruited him to the Federal Theatre Project, a scheme set up by the Roosevelt administration in order to provide work for unemployed actors during the Depression. Given total creative freedom (and also financial freedom, inasmuch as the experiment was subsidized by the government, the only example of such a policy in the history of the United States), Welles made his début on 14 April 1936 with the 'Voodoo *Macbeth*', featuring

Virginia Nicholson in *The Hearts of Age* (1934).

Orson Welles with Arthur Anderson in *Caesar* by the Mercury Theatre troup in 1937.

an all-black cast (or made-up as such: Welles himself took the leading role for the Indianapolis run). The action was transposed to Haiti, with palm and banana trees standing in for Birnam Wood and sixty witch-doctors instead of three witches. In September, he staged a version of Eugène Labiche's *An Italian Straw Hat* (with additional music by Paul Bowles) and, in January 1937, Christopher Marlowe's *Doctor Faustus*. His involvement with the Federal Theatre Project came to an end in June 1937, when the authorities banned the production of *The Cradle Will Rock*, a 'play with music' written by the Marxist composer Marc Blitzstein. Despite a bureaucratic pretext (no new productions could be authorized before 30 June, the end of the fiscal year), the ban was universally interpreted as an act of political censorship designed to suppress an overtly politicized theatre and a play that championed the rights of labour unions. *The Cradle Will Rock* was due to open at the Maxine Elliott Theatre on 16 June, but the venue was closed by the police. Welles and Houseman asked viewers to make their way to the nearby Venice Theatre, where they could at least attend a 'dramatic reading' of the script. Blitzstein himself took to the stage, played the piano and read out the stage directions. The actors (instructed by the unions not to set foot on the stage), sat among the audience and stood in turn to read their lines. The event was extraordinarily successful: the play ran in this form for twelve days and put Welles on the front pages of the newspapers.

Undaunted by the controversy, which effectively terminated their association with the Federal Theatre Project, Welles and Houseman went on to create the Mercury Theatre in July 1937. Welles staged fifty plays under the Mercury banner in two years, including *Caesar*, an adaptation of Shakespeare's *Julius Caesar*; Thomas Dekker's comedy *The Shoemaker's Holiday*; George Bernard Shaw's *Heartbreak House*; *Too Much Johnson*, a comedy by William Gillette (for which Welles shot a 16mm prologue);[3] and Georg Büchner's *Danton's Death*. He then embarked upon *Five Kings*, a massive adaptation of three Shakespearean dramas — *Richard II*, *Henry IV* and *Henry V* — with a running time of five hours and two intervals, but his co-producers, the Theatre Guild, pulled out for financial reasons during the preview tour, thus preventing the official opening in New York. During this period Welles also adapted a lengthy series of literary works for the CBS radio show *The Mercury Theatre on the Air*. One programme, a version of H. G. Wells's *The War of the Worlds*, achieved notoriety when it aired on 30 October 1938. The decision to employ a first-person narrative, giving listeners the impression that they were hearing eyewitness accounts, unleashed a wave of panic throughout the country: more than two million listeners were convinced that Martians had invaded Earth. Welles had hit the headlines once again, and the show attracted the sponsorship of the Campbell Soup Company.[4] Most important, however, was its effect on Hollywood, which began to take a serious interest in Welles's creative genius.

An innovative approach to the performing arts

Leaving aside the whiff of scandal, Welles's frenetic theatre and radio activities were already showing clear signs of an innovative, highly individualistic approach that differed substantially from the conventions of the performing arts.

Foremost among its characteristics was the disappearance of the division between 'high' and

Orson Welles in the 1930s.

Orson Welles with Bernard Herrmann in the 1930s.

Opposite page: Orson Welles in the 1930s.

'low' culture: a Shakespearean drama was accorded the same status as a William Gillette comedy; radio audiences were treated to an adaptation of Stevenson's *Treasure Island* one week and Dickens's *A Tale of Two Cities* the next; Conrad's *Heart of Darkness* was followed by *Passenger to Bali*, from a story by the somewhat less celebrated Ellis St. Joseph. Perhaps the most striking aspect of the Wellesian approach was the creative licence he allowed himself when adapting works of literature. Faithfulness to the text had become a lesser concern when adapting for the stage (he would often pass dialogue from one character to another and shorten lines he thought too long), but the need to capture the radio listener's attention led to a preference for first-person narratives, which tended to strengthen the story and involve the listener in a way that anticipated the use of the voice-off in many of his films. Theatre and radio also provided the opportunity to refine lighting, set design and sound techniques. Spotlights, once simple tools for highlighting characters, the action or specific areas of the set, were transformed into 'elements' of the set design. In *Doctor Faustus*, for example, Welles used the light-absorbing properties of black velvet to isolate the characters, who appeared and disappeared thanks to the vertical columns of light created by velvet cylinders surmounted by lamps. In visual terms, this made it more difficult for the viewer to distinguish between the elements that made up the scene: the black velvet created confusion, cancelling out the spatial coordinates that enabled the eye to get a bearing within the darkness and establish a perspective. Such practices heralded the 'revolution' that would reach its apogee with *Citizen Kane* (1941).

Welles took a similar approach to sound: his productions abandoned the traditional conception of the 'soundtrack' (a musical background to fill moments of silence or accompany selected developments in the story) and instead created a soundscape — a combination of music, noises and dialogue that invested the narrative with new depths. He often instructed his actors to deliver their lines in a way that overlapped, or overlaid the dialogue with deafening sound effects. This was a means of intense aural stimulation; the listener became 'lost' in the soundscape before 'finding' his bearings again, as often happens in real life. He manipulated music written specifically for the stage and radio, tailoring or reducing it according to the needs of his *mise-en-scène*, for he was always alert to the demands of rhythm and concentration. He was also quick to recognize the quality of certain composers, and invited Bernard Herrmann, with whom he had worked at CBS, to join him in Hollywood.

The final element common to Welles's theatrical and radio experience was the creation of a group of actors — the Mercury Players — from whom he sought a certain type of performance. He expected them to relate their work to other aspects of the production and encouraged them to attend rehearsals even when they were not involved in the scene. Body language, a range of identifiable accents and clear pronunciation were also given priority. The names Joseph Cotten, George Coulouris, Agnes Moorehead, Everett Sloane, Erskine Sanford, William Allan, Ray Collins, Paul Stewart, Richard Wilson, Eustace Wyatt, Stefan Schnabel, Edgar Barrier and Frank Readick often featured in the credits for his theatrical productions, radio adaptations and films.

Hollywood

From *Citizen Kane* to *The Lady from Shanghai*

Orson Welles with cinematographer William H. Greene on the set of *It's All True* in 1942.

Heart of Darkness

On 20 July 1939, Welles arrived in Hollywood to sign his first filmmaking contract with RKO, then under the control of George Schaefer.[5] The sixty-three-page document, signed on 21 August, required him to produce, direct, write and act in two films over the following seventeen months. RKO was the least powerful of the five major Hollywood studios,[6] but had perhaps invested more heavily in creativity and was known to welcome innovators. Welles seemed to fit the bill in every respect.

Although still under contract to CBS and committed to *The Campbell Playhouse* series, Welles set to work immediately, selecting Joseph Conrad's *Heart of Darkness*, a novella he had already adapted for CBS (broadcast on 6 November 1938), as his first cinematic venture. The decision to launch his career behind the camera with an acknowledged master-piece of English literature reveals the extent of his ambition, particularly as he intended to empha-size the story's political dimension (the dangers of fascism) at a time when the United States was hoping to maintain its isolationist stance. Moreover, he was determined to revolutionize the way a film was shot: the viewer's eye would be a naive eye, a witness to something absolutely unprecedented.

The screenplay, all 184 pages of it, was ready by 30 November. Welles intervened rather heavily in Conrad's text, constructing the narrative around the meeting with Kurtz, which would constitute the film's dramatic peak.[7] His *Heart of Darkness* would become a quest to fathom the mystery of a power-ful, legendary figure, thus anticipating the structure of *Citizen Kane*.

The film was designed to follow two parallel strands, exploiting the tension between Kurtz and the various characters over whom he exerts his oddly ambivalent power, and at the same time exploring the identification between Kurtz and Marlow. This second strand, underlined but not exactly explicit in Conrad's novella, emerges as a cardinal point in the film, which goes as far as to suggest a physical resem-blance between the two characters. The screenplay also expands the relationship between Kurtz and his fiancée, Elsa, hinting at a kind of emotional tri-angle between Kurtz, Elsa and Marlow. In addition, these changes to the structure of the narrative — which was also transposed to the present in order to heighten its interest — would be emphasized and expanded by a completely new shooting tech-nique. In as much as Conrad's story is a first-person narrative recounted by Marlow, Welles elected to film it through the narrator's eyes. Marlow, voiced by Welles (who would also play Kurtz), would never be a visible presence. The viewer might occasionally see his shadow or his hands as he lit a cigarette, but nothing more. Welles wanted to force the audience to observe the story from Marlow's point of view, through the eyes of an off-screen character. The use of the subjective camera was not unknown in Hollywood, but the idea of shooting an entire film in this way was so revolutionary that RKO eventually pulled the plug on a project whose budget had already exceeded $1 million (Welles intended to film most of it on location in the Florida Everglades or in Panama). The fear of going over budget was exacerbated when war was declared and American studios lost their lucrative European markets.

Robert Montgomery used a similar technique in *The Lady in the Lake* (1947), but the result is disappointing because the subjective camera does not necessarily enable the viewer to identify with the leading character. Welles's approach, however, differed substantially from Montgomery's later attempt in that he sought not only identification, but also a more complex relationship based on attraction and repulsion (we don't always approve of Marlow's behaviour). In addition, the technique could be made to relate organically to the narrative, enhancing its interest by becoming an essential part of it, creating a point of view that would

be both ideological and stylistic. Finally, in order to foster audience identification, Welles came up with the idea of adding an introduction in which the viewer is urged to imagine himself in a series of situations: he is a canary in a cage, he is threatened with a gun, he is condemned to the electric chair, he is an incompetent golfer, and then he is a camera (in effect, every member of the audience would become a spectator and a camera). Welles as narrator would encourage the audience: 'I do want you to understand that you're part of the story. In fact, you are the star.' He thus demonstrated a firm grasp of the psychological links (identification, suspension of belief) between the viewer and what he sees. This concern for the ways in which a film can establish a relationship with its audience would become one of the hallmarks of his work.

Finally, it should be noted that an attentive reading of Conrad's novella reveals that Kurtz, with all his ambiguities, is hardly the positive hero Marlow seems to think he is. On the contrary, he is a monster of violence, and clings to power by means of an ornamental display of human skulls. Welles's screenplay directly addresses the negative side of Kurtz's personality and explicitly compares him to Hitler. It is important to remember that the film should have been made and released at a time when the ambiguity surrounding this subject was far less pronounced. But the negative image of Kurtz, a consequence of shifting the action of the novella to the present day, is nuanced in the screenplay by the greater weight Welles intended to place on the identification between Marlow and Kurtz. In Conrad's narrative, Marlow's fascination with the myth of Kurtz is most clearly felt when he visits Elsa and cannot summon the courage to tell her the truth about her fiancé. Yielding to Kurtz's enigmatic power, he becomes his accomplice, giving him both a soul and the possibility of spiritual salvation. This is precisely

Left and opposite page:
Orson Welles in 1939.

the episode in which Welles departed radically from the original narrative, for he intended to forge a kind of emotional triangle. The Marlow/Kurtz duo, played by the same actor, is in love with the same person. This opens up a dialectic, with the viewer on one side (thanks to the mechanism of identification) and Hitler on the other, and clearly indicates Welles's sympathy for — or rather fascination with — certain personality types.

Welles once said — referring to Quinlan, the corrupt cop in *Touch of Evil* — that one can always feel sympathy for a villain, because sympathy is a human quality, and that's why he was drawn to characters for whom he couldn't hide his disgust. Welles was only interested in powerful characters: men of action, creators and commanders. Even when morally reprehensible, their grandeur filled the screen.

Citizen Kane

Forced to delay his directorial début by the suspension of *Heart of Darkness* (which had at least brought him into contact with cinematographer Gregg Toland), Welles went on to adapt Nicholas Blake's *The Smiler with the Knife*, a thriller in which the heroine pretends to separate from her husband in order to infiltrate a clandestine fascist organization and foil its plans to stage a *coup d'état*. But as RKO deemed the story unworthy of such an eagerly awaited début, Welles began collaborating with screenwriter Herman J. Mankiewicz on an original story.[8] The two men held intense discussions over the concept and narrative structure, and Mankiewicz produced a first draft in March 1940. The film — *American* — would depict the rise and fall of press tycoon Charles Foster Kane. It contained the seeds of the film which, after a further six versions assiduously revised by Welles, would become *Citizen Kane*, the true beginning of his career as a film director. For more than fifty years, critics from all over the world would rank it as one of the greatest, if not the greatest, film in the history of cinema.

Citizen Kane opens with the death of Kane (a role Welles naturally elected to play himself) as he utters his mysterious last word: 'Rosebud'. A newsreel obituary then reviews the highlights of the tycoon's life, his acquisition of newspapers and radio networks, the works of art he amasses in his castle at Xanadu, and his highly contradictory political ideas and choice of company. A journalist is assigned to investigate the meaning of his final word and find out what kind of man he really was. After talking to Kane's second wife, Susan, who appears too depressed to be of any help, the reporter reads the memoirs of the guardian who 'tore' Kane away from his family in order to prepare him for the wealth he was due to inherit. He also seeks out Bernstein, with whom Kane launched *The Inquirer*, and Jedediah Leland, a theatre critic and Kane's closest friend, from whom he learns of the tycoon's first marriage to Emily Norton and the failure of his political ambitions brought about by his relationship with Susan. The reporter returns to Susan, who recalls the nightmare of her career as an opera singer, undertaken simply to please her husband and escape the solitude of life at Xanadu. Finally, he attempts to win the

Ray Collins in *Citizen Kane* (1941).

Orson Welles and Ruth Warrick in *Citizen Kane* (1941).

trust of the butler Raymond, who reveals details of Kane's life after Susan had left him. But the reporter cannot penetrate the enigma of 'Rosebud', although it will be revealed to the audience. As we have seen, there are two strands to the story: on the one hand an often contradictory, effect-filled journalistic reconstruction using tightly edited, strident close-ups and powerful images; and on the other, a series of meetings with witnesses that follows a precise chronology (apart from the two with Susan). These encounters help us to understand aspects of Kane's personality, but shed no light on the 'Rosebud' mystery. The structure of the screenplay indicates that Welles wanted his audience to appreciate a fundamental ambiguity, the impossibility of arriving at any sort of truth, the lack of certainty, factors that constituted the keystone of his entire career. '[...] the meaning of an episode was not inside like a kernel

but outside, enveloping the tale which brought it out only as a glow brings out a haze, in the likeness of one of these misty halos that sometimes are made visible by the spectral illumination of moonshine.' This sentence is from Conrad's *Heart of Darkness*, but for Welles it was a kind of lifelong credo. It describes perfectly the extraordinary intuition that forms the basis of all his work: the illusory nature of images; their delayed decoding; the difficulty of discovering a truth that is not also contradictory; the complexity and ambiguity of whatever appears before our eyes. For Welles, concerns such as these meant that his revolutionary approach could not be confined to the film's narrative structure: it had to involve the totality of cinema by relating form and content, story and images.

The filming of *Citizen Kane* began on 30 July and finished on 23 October 1940, a three-month

Orson Welles in *Citizen Kane* (1941).

shoot that would have a profound effect on the history of cinema. Working closely with cinematographer Gregg Toland and production designer Perry Ferguson, Welles attempted to translate the words of his screenplay into images. He did so in two ways: by appreciably increasing the image's depth of field and by destroying the centrality of perspective. He thus deliberately broke with Hollywood tradition, challenging the tacit agreement that style should play second fiddle to story, or at most conform to it. This would not apply to *Citizen Kane*, in which stylistic choices were transformed into elements that, by helping to tell the story of Charles Foster Kane's life in various ways, were fundamental to a comprehension of the film.

The depth of field Welles and Toland wanted to achieve would offer the viewer a larger expanse of clearly visible space, and consequently a greater choice of objects contained in the same shot. Previously — and even subsequently — the image on the screen had tended to highlight the person or object to which the filmmaker wanted to draw attention, leaving everything surrounding it or behind it indistinct. Welles, however, wanted to experiment with different spatial shots. Toland therefore worked mainly with a Cooke 24mm lens with a very short focal length, which captured a far greater amount of light and gave him a far greater depth of field. The use of Eastman Kodak Super XX film (four times more sensitive than conventional film stock) and a reliance on powerful arc lamps rather than the softer tungsten lamps, substantially enhanced the deep-focus effect of a scene.

This revolutionary approach to lighting brought about other changes, because wide-angle lenses such as the Cooke 24mm enlarged the image

Orson Welles and Joseph Cotten in *Citizen Kane* (1941).

George Coulouris, Harry Shannon, Buddy Swan and Agnes Moorehead in *Citizen Kane* (1941).

both horizontally and vertically, thus forcing the filmmaker to concentrate on the ceilings as well as the other parts of the set. This led to a totally new conception of scenic spaces and camera angles; Welles could use ceilings not only to conceal a larger number of microphones (which enabled him to obtain an unprecedented depth of sound), but also to enhance the dramatic power of a particular scene. A low ceiling that appeared to be 'crushing' or 'imprisoning' the characters heightened the impression of their spatial confinement.

However, the experiment with deep-focus photography should not be interpreted as a quest for greater realism or an opportunity to adapt the camera lens to the human eye, which always brings into focus the space that surrounds it. Welles regarded it as an essential tool for devising a new way of reading the spaces within the shot, for creating an articulated system of spatial references, a new 'symbolic form' with which to subvert the conventions of the medium. This is apparent at the very beginning of *Citizen Kane*, where the narrator (Welles), describing the approach to Xanadu and then the discovery of Kane's death, immediately puts the viewer on his guard and provides a clear demonstration of a new 'form' of cinema.

As the film opens, the travelling shot over the boundaries of the estate seems to unfold in a coherent space. But in the following scene, the fixed shot and constant presence (in the top right-hand corner) of a light inside the looming mass of the castle are contradicted by the left-hand side of the shot, where harmonious dissolves reveal the existence of caged monkeys, a pair of gondolas, a draw bridge and a golf course. By destroying the coherence of the image (if the light inside the castle is always in the same place, then so should be the material in the rest of the shot), Welles also destroys the unity of the visual centre; he allows himself and his viewer total freedom in the organization of the various elements that combine to make up the shot; he constructs space subjectively rather than objectively. And in the following three scenes, which take the viewer from the exterior to the interior of the room where Kane lies dying, and change the point of view even though the architectonic structures that frame the window remain identical and static (the gothic ornamentation on the left-hand side of the shot), all presuppositions about the representation of cinematographic space are discarded.

Who was William Randolph Hearst?

Welles always denied it, but there is no doubt that the protagonist of *Citizen Kane* was inspired by the right-wing press tycoon William Randolph Hearst.

Born on 29 April 1863, Hearst was the son of a senator whose wealth (like Kane's) derived from mining interests, while from his mother he inherited a love of art and the compulsion to collect it. Openly rebelling against his father when at university,

Hearst was twenty-three when he inherited the *San Francisco Examiner*, which he rapidly transformed into a profitable business. Acquiring the *New York Morning Journal* in 1895, he increased its circulation by poaching the most prestigious writers from its rival, the *New York World*. Having founded a newspaper empire, Hearst turned to politics but was unsuccessful in his bids to become mayor of

New York City and governor of New York state.

The parallels with the protagonist of *Citizen Kane* are clear, as is the similarity between Xanadu and La Casa Grande, the estate Hearst built at San Simeon and shared with his mistress, the actress Marion Davies. Like Kane, Hearst tried to promote his mistress's career, but Davies, like Kane's second wife Susan, did not appreciate her

protector's efforts, even when presented with a 110-room beach house in Santa Monica. Hearst died in 1951, by which time his wealth and influence had declined considerably (another point in common with Kane), though he still owned sixteen daily newspapers, two Sunday newspapers and nine magazines.

Hedy Lamarr, William Randolph Hearst and Rita Hayworth in 1942.

Everett Sloane, Orson Welles, Erskine Sanford and Joseph Cotten in *Citizen Kane* (1941).

27

Ray Collins, Dorothy Comingore, Orson Welles and Ruth Warrick in *Citizen Kane* (1941).

In a few seconds, Welles destroys the ten years of work that Hollywood had devoted to constructing in the viewer's imagination a coherent spatial image. *Citizen Kane* demonstrates that a single visual centre does not exist, and proves that the space represented on the screen can be experienced as a three-dimensional phenomenon, so that everything created from the distance between observer and objects can be recuperated. The conscious destruction of a rigidly perspectivist conception of figurative space (in classical Hollywood cinema, soft-focus serves as a more distinctive 'frame' for whatever the camera focuses on) is precisely the means by which the profound stylistic choices of *Citizen Kane* become apparent, and which make the viewer distrust the evidence of his own eyes. Welles's visual grammar is an invitation to uncertainty after years of a cinema in which everything was designed to inculcate certainty and reassurance in the viewer. Throughout the entire film, and indeed in all his subsequent work, Welles takes a central character and constructs around him an increasing number of interwoven reflections, perspectives and connections. The known world disappears. Or more precisely, it appears in a series of disguises, yet seems all the more strange for being exactly the same world. In this way, Welles used his own cinematic alphabet to create a coherent language in which deep focus, montage and composition put paid to the tradition of realist continuity.

Nevertheless, public reaction was disappointing. The difficult, innovative *mise-en-scène* as well as the boycott organized by William Randolph Hearst (Hearst suspected — with good reason — that the Kane character was based on his own, and persuaded many exhibitors to deny the film a screening) did Welles's career no favours. One month after the film's premiere on 1 May 1941, Welles was hard at work on three simultaneous projects — *The Magnificent Ambersons* (1942), *Journey into Fear* (1943) and *It's All True* — but his position at RKO had clearly been weakened, and the tolerance and understanding of its top executives was rapidly running out.

The Magnificent Ambersons

Contractually obliged to make two films for RKO, Welles decided to bring Booth Tarkington's novel *The Magnificent Ambersons* to the screen, having already adapted it for *The Campbell Playhouse* (broadcast 29 October 1939). He worked on the screenplay during the summer of 1941 and began filming it on 28 October. However, in June, RKO had asked him to direct *It's All True*, an anthology picture set in Latin America. The project was designed to improve relations between the United States and its southern neighbours, and to counteract the influence of the Axis powers. Welles optioned the rights to a Robert Flaherty[9] story — *The Captain's Chair* — and sent Norman Foster[10] to Mexico to scout locations for the 'My Friend Bonito' segment. Flaherty would be involved as a screenwriter, while the novelist John Fante would collaborate on the 'Love Story' segment. Duke Ellington was hired to write some of the music for the 'Jam Session' episode.

In April 1941, RKO had also asked Welles to play a secondary role in *Journey into Fear*, a noir film set in Turkey and based on the novel by Eric Ambler. He offered to produce the film as well. How would he cope with so many commitments? He did his best, with results that were undoubtedly unforeseen: in order to achieve greater financial freedom and bolster his bank account (although much of the work was still at the development stage), he agreed to relinquish some of the power

Anne Baxter, Tim Holt, Agnes Moorehead and Don Dillaway in *The Magnificent Ambersons* (1942).

he had gained on his arrival at RKO, particularly in the matter of the final cut.[11] Welles would experience the consequences of this renunciation far sooner than he had imagined.

The Magnificent Ambersons chronicles the decline of the upper-class Amberson family as America enters the twentieth century, and the parallel social rise of the middle-class Eugene Morgan, a shrewd inventor and future captain of the automobile industry whom Isabel Amberson had once rejected as a suitor. The passage of time and the fact that the former lovers have lost their spouses does not improve matters, for Isabel's son George, an inveterate snob, once again prevents their marriage, and also represses his feelings for Eugene's daughter Lucy.

Reserving the narrator's role for himself, Welles cast several Mercury Players — Joseph Cotten (Eugene Morgan), Agnes Moorehead (the jealous old maid Aunt Fanny) and Ray Collins (Uncle Jack, Isabel's brother) — and enlisted outsiders such as Dolores Costello (Isabel), Tim Holt (George Amberson) and Anne Baxter (the young Lucy). However, finding a cameraman and a production designer proved more difficult as Gregg Toland was unavailable and Perry Ferguson had gone to work for MGM. Ferguson was replaced by Mark-Lee Kirk, perhaps less inventive but still an expert production designer. However, Welles, also working on *Journey into Fear*, and with *It's All True* on the horizon, was not entirely happy with the young cinematographer Stanley Cortez, whom he found too slow.

Burdened with so many commitments, Welles was eventually forced to agree to something he would never have countenanced in the past: on 6 January 1942, obliged to divide his time between *The Magnigicent Ambersons* and his other tasks as actor and producer on *Journey into Fear*, he delegated the shooting of several *Ambersons* scenes to a second unit (a common practice in Hollywood), and thus lost overall control of the film's visual and artistic cohesion. Moreover, while the editing had been entrusted to Robert Wise,[12] who had already demonstrated his skills on *Citizen Kane*, Welles could only participate in the process via telephone, cable and radio, as he had arrived in Rio de Janeiro on 8 February to film

Tim Holt, Agnes Moorehead and Dolores Costello in *The Magnificent Ambersons* (1942).

Opposite page: Agnes Moorehead and Tim Holt
in *The Magnificent Ambersons* (1942).

Orson Welles with Joseph Cotten and Dolores Costello
on the set of *The Magnificent Ambersons* (1942).

the carnival for one of the three confirmed segments of *It's All True*. Given his distance from Hollywood, Welles was also unable to address the misgivings of RKO's executives, who had previewed *The Magnificent Ambersons* and found that audiences disliked its sombre and sometimes despairing atmosphere. George Schaefer authorized chief camera operator Nicholas Musuraca and assistant director Fred Fleck to shoot new scenes to cover the numerous cuts the studio had imposed. The first cut ran for 131 minutes, but the version that finally reached the screen on 10 July 1942 ran for only 88 minutes.

What remains of Welles's art in this truncated version? Without doubt, the masterly and very modern manipulation of cinematographic space and time. The ballroom scene at the Amberson residence, a synthesis of conflicting relations between diverse characters, and their 'displacement' in various parts of the set and frame (at the top and bottom of staircases, in the foreground of the ballroom and some distance from it) is still a very powerful example of the science of *mise-en-scène*. The same can also be said for certain scenes in which George courts Lucy, especially the lateral travelling shot of the drive in the carriage. But it is clear that Welles had envisaged an entirely different rhythm for the film, one that placed greater emphasis on the contrast between the 'old' world represented by the Ambersons and the 'modern' world of factories and the industrial degradation that accompanies progress. Similarly, the ending should have been very different in tone. But despite studio interference, the film has an underlying, almost secret charm, like that of a rather faded portrait of a society eroded to the point of extinction. Strong contrasts between light and shadow suggest a universe and an era too superficially rejected and forgotten, although a 'voice' still lingers on, an impression enhanced by the credits, which are not displayed but spoken by the off-screen voice of Welles himself. 33

Everett Sloane, Joseph Cotten, Frank Puglia
and Orson Welles in *Journey into Fear* (1943).

Following pages: Dolores del Río, Hans Conried,
Joseph Cotten and Everett Sloane in *Journey into Fear* (1943).

Journey into Fear

As Welles had to leave for Rio he could not attend the entire shoot of *Journey into Fear*. Norman Foster, working on the 'My Friend Bonito' segment of *It's All True* in Mexico, was hastily recalled to Hollywood and given the job of directing the Eric Ambler story. The film follows the fortunes of an American arms engineer, Howard Graham, who is sent on a mission to Istanbul and becomes the target of Nazi assassins. The mysterious Colonel Haki, head of the Turkish secret services, comes to his aid and puts him on a ship bound for Russia, but its passengers include the Nazi killer Banat as well as a group of bizarre and shady individuals, and the mild-mannered Graham is forced to become a man of action.

Journey into Fear was released on 12 February 1943, and credits Welles as producer, screenwriter (with Joseph Cotten, who also played Graham) and actor in the role of Colonel Haki (a character with a deliberate resemblance to Stalin). He received no director's credit, but his influence in that capacity is clear. Some of the film's participants have recalled his involvement, and his imprint is apparent in many scenes (including the final pursuit of Graham on the hotel ledge) and in certain fundamental stylistic choices, such as the play of light and shadow on the actors' faces as they move through vast areas of darkness on the set. The choice of actors was also totally Wellesian: besides the usual Mercury Players (Joseph Cotten, Agnes Moorehead, Everett Sloane, Eustace Wyatt, Stefan Schnabel, Frank Readick, Edgar Barrier), the film featured Jack Moss, Mercury's business manager, as the killer Banat, and Dolores del Río (Welles's new companion following his divorce from Virginia Nicholson in 1940) as Josette, the dancer and temptress Graham meets on the boat. Some of the minor and major 'bits of business' do little to enhance the film's quality; although intriguing in a formal sense, the film is less successful in terms of content, which, while hinting at a certain psychological disorientation, is notable for a taste for fancy dress that borders on the farcical.

35

Above and opposite page: *It's All True* (shot 1941–2).

It's All True

Given all the tribulations Welles had encountered when making *The Magnificent Ambersons* and *Journey into Fear*, his enforced absences from the Hollywood sets and their dire consequences, it was not unreasonable to hope that with *It's All True* he would at last be allowed total creative freedom. But following the attack on Pearl Harbor on 7 December 1941, the film became a priority for the Office of the Coordinator of Inter-American Affairs (CIAA), headed by Nelson Rockefeller, which pushed for its completion and pumped $300,000 into the project. The need to improve relations with Latin American countries led to the selection of three segments from all those Welles had prepared: 'My Friend Bonito', in which a boy befriends a bull, 'Four Men

on a Raft', a re-enactment of a voyage made by four poor Brazilian fishermen (*jangadeiros*) to Rio to petition president and dictator Getúlio Vargas for better conditions, and 'The Story of Samba', a celebration of Brazil's musical culture and folklore.

Welles arrived in Rio on 8 February 1942, six days before the opening of the carnival he planned to film. The lack of technical preparation, absence of screenplay and logistical difficulties were overcome with the enthusiastic assistance of the Brazilian army, which supplied the searchlights required for the Technicolor night scenes. But there were further problems, particularly with the *jangadeiros* segment. The Brazilian authorities and the CIA feared that the director, a political progressive, would devote too much footage to the country's black and mixed

It's All True (shot 1941–2).

race populations and neglect the need to celebrate its cordial relations with the United States. Tragedy struck with the drowning of Jacaré, the fishermen's leader and hero of the segment. Changes occurred at the top of RKO, where the ousting of George Schaefer and his replacement by the more pragmatic Charles Koerner dealt a decisive blow to Welles's hopes. The crew and equipment were repatriated, and Welles himself was ordered back to Hollywood at the end of July. He left Brazil having shot 70 hours of colour footage and 17 hours in black and white, all of which ended up in RKO's vault. The footage was rediscovered in 1985 and used in 1993 by Richard Wilson, Myron Meisel and Bill Krohn for *It's All True: Based on an Unfinished Film by Orson Welles*. Their film is both a documentary account of the work in Brazil, including interviews and footage dating from that period, and a restoration of part of the original material

Politics

Welles held progressive views and was not averse to personal involvement in politics. The choices he had made when working for the Federal Theatre Project, culminating in the suspension of *The Cradle Will Rock*, had already constituted a clear political stance. But it was mainly in the 1940s, at a time when the United States was still tempted by isolationism, that he used his popularity and ideas to oppose fascism in all its forms.

Along with many other actors, including Charles Boyer and Betsy Blair (then married to Gene Kelly), Welles joined the committee to defend the seventeen Mexican-Americans who were accused, particularly by Hearst group newspapers, of involvement in the killing of José Díaz (known as the 'Sleepy Lagoon murder'). He was also an enthusiastic participant in Franklin D. Roosevelt's Good Neighbor Policy (which damaged his relations with the Hollywood establishment and led to his move to Latin America). Welles fervently adopted the ideas and initiatives of his friend and producer Louis Dolivet, a French national who had fled occupied France for the United States, where he founded the Free World organization in an attempt to stimulate international cooperation. At a meeting organized by Dolivet in New York in October 1943, Welles rubbed shoulders with British ambassador Harold Butler, Chinese ambassador Wei Tao-Ming, the Spanish Republican government's foreign minister, Julio Álvarez del Vayo, and US Marine Colonel Evans Carlson. He also contributed articles to Free World's monthly bulletin, some of which appeared on its front page (his final piece, 'Now or Never', dealt directly with the atomic bomb and the possibility of mass destruction, a fate he claimed could be avoided only by the immediate establishment of a new democratic world order). The decision to campaign for a fourth term for Roosevelt in 1944 seemed to be the next logical step. Although his new wife, Rita Hayworth, was expecting a child, Welles accompanied Roosevelt on several stages of the election campaign, directly addressing the crowds and often helping to write his speeches.

This was the period that gave rise to the famous anecdote according to which Welles advised the unsteady Roosevelt to enter a venue from the left instead of the right: 'Mr President, you've never gone wrong when you've turned left.' According to biographer Barbara Leaming, Welles was tempted to abandon film-making for a more active political career, but was blocked by the hostile attitude of Roosevelt's wife, Eleanor.

However, this setback did nothing to modify his political views. During his 'exile' in Europe, he was monitored by the FBI, which regarded him as a dangerous communist. Their suspicions seemed justified when Welles met Palmiro Togliatti, head of the Italian Communist Party, the largest such party in the West, in Rome on 8 December 1947. Welles had dinner with Togliatti and three journalists (including *Time* magazine's correspondent), but the conversation centred on culture rather than politics, and even the FBI was eventually forced to admit that *Citizen Kane*'s director was no dangerous purveyor of anti-American sentiments.

comprising the complete but silent 'Four Men on a Raft', several sequences from 'My Friend Bonito' and a few scenes from 'The Story of Samba'. The power of the images, their clear echoes of Eisenstein and references to Murnau, demonstrate Welles's desire to abandon cinematic conventions and develop a new aesthetic. Watching them today induces a kind of sadness, for *It's All True* was the first of many films that he never managed to complete.

Edward G. Robinson, Richard Long, Loretta Young, Martha Wentworth, Orson Welles, Philip Merivale and Byron Keith in *The Stranger* (1946).

The Stranger

Back in the United States, Welles was faced with the task of restoring his credibility as a producer and director — if not his credibility as an artist — which had been tested so severely towards the end of his association with RKO. The Hollywood establishment had not exactly slammed the door in his face, but it expected him to relinquish his dream of producing and directing and devote his energy to appearing in front of the camera. This was no idle period, however, given his work for CBS radio, the newspaper columns and speaking engagements, the campaigning in support of the war effort, the recordings for Decca (readings from famous texts, including passages from Pericles and the Bible), and a new romance with Rita Hayworth. Resigning himself to acting for a while, he played Rochester opposite Joan Fontaine in Robert Stevenson's *Jane Eyre* (1943) and John MacDonald/Erik Kessler opposite Claudette Colbert in Irving Pichel's *Tomorrow Is Forever* (1946). Both films were produced by

William Goetz, who offered Welles the Franz Kindler/Charles Rankin role in *The Stranger* (1946) and also asked him to direct the picture. The story follows investigator Wilson's efforts to track down Franz Kindler, a Nazi war criminal thought to have gone to ground in a small Connecticut town, where, assuming the identity of Charles Rankin, he teaches at the high school and has married the judge's daughter, Mary. Wilson releases and trails one of Kindler's old comrades, whom the suspect subsequently murders. Wilson finally convinces Mary of her husband's guilt, and she agrees to collaborate in his downfall.

Goetz hired Sam Spiegel as producer, and Welles had to prove that he was still a trustworthy director who could bring in a picture on schedule and within budget. He wanted to make the investigator a woman and shoot a prologue in South America in order to provide a context for the pursuit of Nazi war criminals, but these suggestions were rejected, as were his plans to enhance the small-town atmosphere by filming the exteriors on location. He was allowed to use documentary footage of concentration camps (Wilson shows them to Mary in order to enlist her aid), the first time such material had appeared in a fiction film. But apart from that his only freedom of action concerned the photography, which he entrusted to the little-known cameraman Russell Metty. Metty's exceptionally fluid transitions from shadow to clarity endow the characters with a stark emphasis and convey an impression of extreme instability.

Although *The Stranger* was a commercial success, especially given the presence of stars Edward G. Robinson and Loretta Young, the film nevertheless constitutes an anomaly in Welles's filmography. Rankin lacks the stature of a Kane or a Hank Quinlan; awareness of his evil nature has to be encouraged by contrasting him with the pettiness of the town's inhabitants. The almost hysterical obduracy and incomprehension of Mary, the naivety of the old ladies hanging on to Rankin's every word, and the callowness of the high school pupils — all help to create a more ambiguous provincial community than the kind traditionally represented by Hollywood, but the film displays little of the complexity and analytical depth Welles achieved in other films. Only the denouement in the baroque clock tower, a distinctly Mittel-European edifice with its bells clanging in the otherwise neo-classical atmosphere of New England, suggests the visual and narrative possibilities he might have exploited had he been allowed more freedom.

Orson Welles and Loretta Young
in *The Stranger* (1946).

Following pages: Orson Welles and Rita Hayworth
in *The Lady from Shanghai* (1947).

The Lady from Shanghai

An opportunity seemed to arise in the spring of 1946, when Welles, needing to repay the $25,000 Columbia's president Harry Cohn had lent him to finance rehearsals for a colossal musical production of *Around the World in Eighty Days*, agreed to direct Rita Hayworth (now almost his ex-wife) in *The Lady from Shanghai*, an adaptation of Sherwood King's dark thriller *If I Die Before I Wake*. The film would keep him busy from October 1946 to February 1947. It was released in Europe at the end of 1947, but not until June 1948 in the United States.

Having saved the beautiful Elsa from an assault, sailor Michael O'Hara is offered a job on the yacht owned by her husband, the lawyer Arthur Bannister. O'Hara accepts the proposition put to him by Bannister's associate George Grisby,

to pretend to kill Grisby so that he can start a new life. O'Hara hopes to run away with Elsa thanks to the money promised by Grisby, but naturally the scheme goes awry and he finds himself accused of two murders. Bannister undertakes his defence, but when O'Hara realizes that his lawyer's aim is to prove him guilty, he escapes from the courtroom and takes refuge in San Francisco's Chinatown, where he eventually discovers who masterminded the trap into which he has fallen.

Despite all the means placed at his disposal, Welles was unable to fulfil his hope of enhancing a genre picture by shooting most of it on location. He did succeed in exploiting certain aspects of Acapulco and San Francisco, but Cohn's insistence on maximum exposure for his biggest box-office draw obliged him to resort to a great many

Everett Sloane and Orson Welles in *The Lady from Shanghai* (1947).

close-ups and continuity shots so that the image of Rita Hayworth filled the screen at every opportunity. Welles was thus thwarted in his attempt to anchor the story in a realistic milieu and depict the corrosive influence of tourism on Mexico (indicated by the stupid jokes cracked by the tourists who interrupt the walk taken by O'Hara and Grisby), and its indelible poverty (as in the scenes of working-class life that form the background to the meeting between Elsa and O'Hara). The dialogue, however, alerts the audience to O'Hara's political past as a volunteer for the Spanish Republican cause and his part in the execution of a spy. But, above all, Welles seized the chance to settle accounts with Hollywood and the American dream: he strips the *femme fatale* figure of all traces of romanticism. The film ends with a devastating gesture of contempt for

star status as the hero walks away from the dying Rita Hayworth, who, to the consternation of her fans, had been forced to have her hair cut short and dyed blonde for the part. The other characters fare no better; O'Hara compares them to sharks, eating each other, individuals with an insatiable lust for money. Although the presentation of the hero is a little too schematic at times (he seems too naive, despite the ironic voice-off commentary), the film's strength lies in a series of scenes — O'Hara's courting of Elsa in front of the aquarium and the octopus pool, the Chinese theatre, the hall of mirrors in which the final shoot-out takes place — that combine exceptional visual power with a bitter symbolism and a disillusioned lesson in morality.

Welles thus managed to overcome the restrictions imposed by the studio and return to the

Rita Hayworth and Orson Welles in *The Lady from Shanghai* (1947).

source of his own inspiration, transforming the obsessions at the origin of his career as a director — the destructive power wielded by the studios and also the possibility of smashing the medium's conventions — into the keystone of his relationship with cinema. It was not by chance that all his previous films had been genre films, or that in each case he had used his genius to subvert their conventions. This applies to the films noirs *The Lady from Shanghai* and *Journey into Fear*, the police thriller *The Stranger*, and to *The Magnificent Ambersons*, which belongs to one of Hollywood's favourite literary genres, the family saga that unfolds over several generations. Moreover, his first film, *Citizen Kane*, is clearly related to the journalistic comedy, one of the most popular genres of the 1930s, a point made by the American critic Pauline Kael in 'Raising Kane', a controversial essay published 1971. Kael ignores the film's dramatic component, not to mention Welles's visual contribution, but the essay makes it clear that his characteristic approach, his selection of a canonical genre and intention to destroy it from within, dates back to his first film.

The films noirs Welles directed surpass those of Fritz Lang and Billy Wilder, for he was not content with calling into question the cultural foundations of American society (matriarchy, the obsession with a career, faith in law and order): he irremediably confuses our mental logical coordinates, the factors that govern human perception and emotion. In the Wellesian universe, even primary sensations are deceptive. Thus his journey to the heart of the genre film (and to the heart of Hollywood) inevitably took him elsewhere: to Europe ('Europe for me is more necessity than choice'), to Shakespearean theatre and to the literature of Kafka, where the methods of artistic expression that had obsessed him for years would no longer be stifled by the rigidities of the studio system and the conventions of filmmaking.

Orson Welles and Jeanette Nolan
(the Queen) in *MacBeth* (1948).

Shakespeare
Macbeth, Othello

Macbeth

Welles approached Shakespeare by gradually increasing his distance from the texts. But this was a two-way process: the greater the liberties he took with the plays, the closer he came to their true spirit. His adaptations for the cinema include an interpretation of *Macbeth* that respects the verse structure, an almost nineteenth-century rereading of *Othello*, and a highly personal interweaving of Shakespearean characters and his own experiences of life in *Chimes at Midnight*. Shakespeare was a constant presence in Welles's life, to the extent that, as his biographer Joseph McBride has rightly observed, whenever he wanted to find himself artistically, he returned to Shakespeare's plays.

As regards *Macbeth*, Welles decided to combine theatre and cinema, his two great passions. Alert to the need to keep costs down and shoot in as short a period as possible, he decided to stage the play at the University Theatre in Salt Lake City, then film the production for Republic Pictures,[13] using the same cast. Harnessing the opportunities offered by 'fringe' theatre and a studio specializing in B films, he regained, albeit briefly, the freedom that Hollywood had curtailed. In retrospect, it could be argued that after the slap he had received from

'Profile of Orson Welles' by Jean Cocteau

Orson Welles's *Macbeth* is a *film maudit*, in the noble sense of the word, such as we used it to light the beacon of the Festival at Biarritz.

Orson Welles's *Macbeth* leaves the spectator deaf and blind and I can well believe that the people who like it (and I am proud to be one) are few and far between. Welles shot the film very quickly after numerous rehearsals. In other words, he wanted it to retain a certain theatrical style, as a proof that cinematography can put any work of art under its magnifying glass and dispense with the rhythm commonly supposed to be that of cinema. [...] Orson Welles's *Macbeth* has a kind of crude, irreverent power. Clad in animal skins like motorists at the turn of the century, horns and cardboard crowns on their heads, his actors haunt the corridors of some dream-like subway, an abandoned coal mine, and ruined cellars oozing with water. Not a single shot is left to chance. The camera is always placed just where destiny itself would observe its victims. Sometimes we wonder in what period this nightmare is unfolding, and when, for the first time, we see Lady Macbeth, before the camera moves back to situate her, it is almost a woman in modern dress that we are seeing, reclining on a fur-covered divan before the telephone.

In the role of Macbeth, Orson Welles proves himself to be a remarkable tragedian, and if the Scottish accent imitated by Americans may be unbearable to English ears, I confess that it did not disturb me and that it would not have disturbed me even if I had a perfect command of English, since we have no reason not to expect that strange monsters express themselves in a monstrous language in which the words of Shakespeare nevertheless remain his words.

In short, I am a poor judge and a better judge than others in that, without any difficulty, I could concentrate on the plot alone and my discomfort arose from it instead of from a faulty accent. This film, withdrawn by Welles from the competition in Venice and screened by *Objectif 49*, in 1949, at the Maison de la Chimie, has everywhere met with the same kind of opposition. It epitomizes the character of Orson Welles, who disregards convention and whose weaknesses, to which the public clings as to a life preserver, have alone afforded him any success. Sometimes his boldness is blessed with such good fortune that the public is willing to be seduced, as for example, in the scene from *Citizen Kane* when Kane wrecks the bedroom, or in that of the maze of mirrors from *The Lady from Shanghai*.

And yet, after the syncopated rhythm of *Citizen Kane*, the public expected a succession of syncopes and was disappointed by the calm beauty of *The Magnificent Ambersons*. It was easier for the soul to go astray in the labyrinthine penumbra taking us from the strange image of the little millionaire, not unlike Louis XIV, to the hysterics of his aunt.

This is an extract from Jean Cocteau, 'Profile of Orson Welles' in André Bazin, *Orson Welles: A Critical View*, tr. Jonathan Rosenbaum, Elm Tree Books, London, 1978.

Hollywood, Welles's return to directing with the barbarous and vengeful *Macbeth* revealed a desire for independence and revenge that could be achieved only by deliberately turning his back on the major studios and their star system. *Macbeth*, with its papier mâché sets, dry ice and verse dialogue, was guaranteed to offend the solid commercial sense of the studios, but it enabled Welles to return to his roots as a director and to reclaim an independence that was as existential as it was creative.

Welles, as usual, offered his own interpretation of the play. He insisted on emphasizing the determination with which Macbeth (a role he naturally reserved for himself) decides to rebel against the forces of evil — and of the past — that had dragged him into an ever darker abyss. He transformed Shakespeare's savage portrayal of a man's lust for power and a woman's treacherous intrigues into an original meditation on the birth of culture and history, placing at the heart of his interpretation the conflict between the chaos of supernatural forces (embodied by the three witches) and the new order announced by Christianity. To this end, he invented a character that does not exist in Shakespeare — a 'Holy Father' (played by Alan Napier), who serves to stress certain fundamental narrative links.

While such artistic licence may have dismayed purists, the studio heads were infuriated when Welles 'fled' to Europe after the shoot, thereby prolonging the editing, which he would have to supervise from Italy while acting in Gregory Ratoff's film, *Black Magic*. *Macbeth* had taken only twenty-one days to shoot (23 June — 17 July 1947), but the editing process would not be completed until the summer of 1948! A limited trial run in October 1948 was badly received. Audiences did not like Shakespeare's verses delivered in a very heavy Scottish accent, full of rolling 'r's and other guttural sounds that Welles considered an essential departure from the emphatic diction traditionally employed on the stage. Republic ordered him to redub much of the dialogue and shorten certain scenes. When *Macbeth* was eventually released in 1950, its length had been trimmed from 107 to 86 minutes.

Meanwhile, Welles had become more and more European. He had realized that his fame was much more appreciated on the other side of the Atlantic, where it was also easier to find work as an actor (Cesare Borgia in Henry King's *Prince of Foxes*, Harry Lime in Carol Reed's *The Third Man*), and as a director. Indeed, by September 1948 he was already at work on *Othello*, with himself in the title role and Lea Padovani as Desdemona.

Above and opposite page: Orson Welles and Suzanne Cloutier in *Othello* (1952).

Othello

Given the precarious financial position of Scalera Studios, the film's original Italian backer, Welles was forced to look for funds elsewhere. He also needed more actors, including a new Desdemona, as his relationship with Padovani had ended. He embarked on a very personal odyssey through a series of locations in the Mediterranean, which ended only in March 1950, when he managed to overcome the complexities of his own acting commitments for film and radio, those of his cast (Micheál MacLiammóir as Iago, Robert Coote as Roderigo, first Betsy Blair and finally Suzanne Cloutier as Desdemona), fundraising and location scouting (Venice, the Moroccan towns of Essaouira and Safi, Rome, Tuscany, Viterbo, Venice again and finally Morocco). The shoot thus had to be a highly flexible affair. The editors would later patch together individual shots and manipulate the variety of camera set-ups to hide the existence of so many disparate locations. Filters and high contrast images would also disguise the fact that the film had been shot by three different cameramen — Anchise Brizzi, G. R. Aldo and George Fanto. Alexandre Trauner, a highly creative production designer, made the most of his limited resources, using fog, the play of light, steam and shadows to merge the hotchpotch of locations and sets. That the film is a genuine *tour de force* is a testament to Welles's ability to coordinate the entire project with extraordinary precision (the scripts and the voluminous notes he wrote for his collaborators refute the allegation that the film had been improvised from day to day). This attention to detail extended to post-production, and editing continued right up

Othello

We speak of the 'aesthetics of poverty', but perhaps the 'aesthetics of necessity' would be more appropriate in this context. Welles was never discouraged by budgetary restrictions but, rather, exploited them to his advantage. In *Othello*, the Turkish bath scene featuring Iago, Roderigo and Cassio demonstrates this yet again. Although Shakespeare set the scene in the streets of Cyprus, the costumes ordered from the Italian firm Peruzzi had not reached Essaouira (they had not been paid for), so Welles decided to set it in a steam bath, where the characters would need nothing but towels. On another occasion, Alexandre Trauner designed a set in one of the towers of a fortress, yet Welles was able to avoid emphasizing its spatial constrictions by fragmenting the shot breakdown, alternating between very tight pans and close shots or close-ups of the principal actors. Limited light (and the lack of lamps) forced him to accentuate the contrasts between light and shadow, transforming dark areas into a visual leitmotif of the scene. Darkness becomes an aesthetic metaphor for the ambiguity of Iago and his plot (to use Roderigo's passion for Desdemona and presumed rivalry with Cassio in order to dupe the former into murdering the latter). Vertical and horizontal shadows are used as 'slats' to delimit and confine space. The camera, whether almost 'glued' to the actors' faces or prowling the boundaries of the set, also serves to enhance the conspiratorial atmosphere of the scene. The framework is almost that of a thriller, which literally explodes when Roderigo, concealed beneath a slatted floor is run through by Iago: Welles did not have the special effects required to film the murder scene, but during the editing he overlaid the image of a brightly illuminated sword that 'slices through' a zone of darkness in which we intermittently perceive small but lighter fissures. This was an ideal way to indicate a murder without showing it; the final two shots of water trickling from the flooring seal the scene with a perverse catharsis.

Orson Welles in *Othello* (1952).

Opposite page: Orson Welles and Suzanne Cloutier in *Othello* (1952).

to the film's screening at the Cannes Film Festival in 1952, almost four years after the first scenes were shot in Venice in September 1948.

Othello, the product of years of work and financial wrangling, became for Welles the means by which he could assert, with total conviction, his decision to reject Hollywood's facile dependence on cinematic realism. The richness of Shakespeare's text, the variety of readings and interpretations it offered, enabled Welles to reject naturalism and opt for a more creative *mise-en-scène*. Perhaps a less chequered production history would have resulted in a different version of the conflict between Othello and Iago. But the brilliance of the editing, which matches a square in Torcello with a Moroccan rampart, is not the trick of a filmmaker in want of materials; it is the best — perhaps the only — way to endow all the disparate elements of the décor with an authentic dramatic rhythm, to concretize

to some extent the possibility of an atmosphere that itself becomes an element of the tragedy. In order to do this, Welles had to step back from Shakespeare's narrative richness, suppress almost all the Venetian scenes and elevate Iago to the status of an authentic 'co-hero' (as in Arrigo Boito's opera version). His version of the drama of the Moor foregrounds the conflict between two cultures and two forms of conduct rather than the psychological trajectory that drives a jealous husband to madness and murder. His *mise-en-scène* is imposing and majestic, as the film's opening and closing scenes clearly demonstrate; 'his' Othello — a towering, tragic figure — is an instinctive and uncultured individual at war with a civilization from which he feels hopelessly excluded. In this 're-reading' of *Othello*, the world created by Shakespeare becomes a representation of Welles's obsessions, and their two worlds intermingle and merge both ideologically and aesthetically.

Welles the actor

Perhaps only the Italian film-maker Vittorio De Sica could lay claim to as rich a career both in front of the camera and behind it. Welles acted in all his own films except *The Magnificent Ambersons* (for which he provided the narration), and in more than a hundred others, either in person or as a voice, either as the central character or in a self-indulgent secondary role. But his presence was always unforgettable.

At the beginning of his career his acting talents seemed inseparable from his gifts as a director (or at least his gift for 'directing himself'). Thus his participation in *Journey into Fear*, supposedly confined to producing and acting, actually extended beyond those responsibilities: he directed his own scenes as Colonel Haki, as well as some of the most important sequences. His talent for self-direction is also evident in *Touch of Evil*.

Moving to Europe in order to escape Hollywood's repressive atmosphere, he continued to regard himself as an inviolable unit: he was an actor, but he was perfectly capable of directing himself. His influence was so powerful that other directors, even independent spirits with strong views of their own, found it hard to resist. While he probably never attempted to influence the way Carol Reed shot *The Third Man* (1949), Reed's handling of the Harry Lime character, the black-market hustler played by Welles, is clearly 'Wellesian', and lends credence to the long-held belief that some degree of 'co-direction' was involved. Welles often accepted roles in order to pay off old debts (advances never repaid, favours that had to be returned) or meet pressing financial obligations. He never forgot the advances he received during his stay in Italy in the 1950s, money for films that were never shot, undertaken with reluctance or manipulated to suit his own agenda (acting in Ferdinando Baldi and Richard Pottier's *David and Goliath*, 1960, he managed to delay the filming of his own scenes – for which he naturally rewrote the dialogue – until 5 p.m. so that most of his day could be devoted to shooting his own *Don Quixote*). Even so, many of his performances, including brief appearances and cameo roles, are delightful and unforgettable, especially Father Mapple in John Huston's *Moby Dick* (1956), Will Varner in Martin Ritt's *The Long, Hot Summer* (1958), the idle director in Pier Paolo Pasolini's 'La Ricotta' (1963), Colonel Cascorro in Giulio Petroni's *Tepepa* (1968), General Dreedle in Mike Nichols' *Catch-22* (1970) and the disturbing Cassavius in Harry Kümel's *Malpertuis* (1971).

In all of these roles Welles never failed to deploy his talents as a 'performer' and indulge his taste for disguises (the countless false noses and beards, the improbable make-up as a Tartar and a Viking, as Tiresias and Benjamin Franklin). He took great pleasure in astonishing everybody by his willingness to appear in B, C or even Z movies, but every performance was an example of a unique actor's art.

Left: Orson Welles in
Carol Reed's *The Third Man* (1949).

Right: Orson Welles in
Mike Nichols' *Catch 22* (1970).

Opposite page: Orson Welles
in Pier Paolo Pasolini's 'La ricotta' (1963).

Europe

From *Mr. Arkadin* to *Filming Othello*

Orson Welles in *Mr. Arkadin* (1955).

Following page: Robert Arden
and Paola Mori in *Mr. Arkadin* (1955).

Mr. Arkadin

Lauded at the 1952 Cannes Film Festival, where *Othello* was awarded the Palme d'Or (an honour shared with Renato Castellani's *Two Cents Worth of Hope*), Welles continued to take on acting roles, not all of which were English-language productions (he co-starred with the comic actor Totò in Steno's *L'uomo, la bestia e la virtù*). He also contemplated a return to the theatre, but soon found himself behind the camera again, directing *Mr. Arkadin*, produced by his friend and political mentor Louis Dolivet. The film was also known as *Confidential Report*; the existence of two titles, indicating that there are different versions of the film, is already enough to alert us to the adversity that beset this new venture.

Welles plays Gregory Arkadin, one of the world's wealthiest men. Pathologically protective of his daughter (Paola Mori, later to become Welles's third wife), Arkadin claims to suffer from amnesia, and hires Guy Van Stratten, a shady adventurer who once attempted to blackmail him, in order to 'rediscover' his past. Van Stratten discovers the source of Arkadin's wealth (an international prostitution ring) and realizes that he has actually been hired to track down anyone who knows about this shameful past so that they can be eliminated. Once all the witnesses have been taken care of, Van Stratten himself will have to die.

Shot haphazardly in various European locations over an eight-month period — from January to August 1954 — the film severely tested Welles's friendship with Dolivet, who accused his director of making too many changes to the screenplay and disregarding the production schedule in order to suit the needs of the cast.[14] Further problems arose when shares in the film had to be sold to various foreign distributors in order to fund the rest of the shoot. The copies Welles edited in various parts of Europe thus became 'hostages' in the hands of various co-producers (Spanish, English, French and Swiss). These associates, naturally concerned to get their money back, ended up by circulating a provisional version of the film (sometimes with several inappropriate revisions) in their home territories. By the time of its British premiere in August 1955, there were at least seven different versions of *Mr. Arkadin* (or *Confidential Report*) in existence, each distributor having a different opinion on the title, the running time and the editing (versions varied between 96 and 105 minutes).

However, *Mr. Arkadin* is still a potentially great film. Welles systematically distorts both image and

Grégoire Aslan (on the floor) and Patricia Medina in *Mr. Arkadin* (1955).

Following pages: Mischa Auer and Robert Arden in *Mr. Arkadin* (1955).

narrative, the décor style veering between the baroque and the fairground. Oblique images destroy traditional perspective (the splendid murder scene in the port of Naples). Wide angles and close-ups of ravaged, monstrous faces constitute the hallmarks of a story that unravels into a series of digressions. Bolstered by an extraordinary cast of character actors — Akim Tamiroff, Michael Redgrave, Mischa Auer, Katina Paxinou, Suzanne Flon, Peter Van Eyck, Gert Fröbe — secondary episodes take precedence over the main story. Welles, decked out in an obviously false beard and an equally fake nose, dominates the proceedings and gives himself an unforgettable scene — the tale of the frog and the scorpion — which too many filmmakers have since felt obliged to reprise or refer to in order to establish their credentials as bona fide cinephiles.[15]

As always, problems arose in the editing room. By this time it was obvious that Welles regarded the editing as the most vital part of the filmmaking process, but it inevitably led to conflicts with producers, who tended to believe that once the film was in the can, most of the work had been done. Moreover, by the mid-1950s his creative instincts had been aroused by the possibilities of television. He considered it a more rapid means of communication, more malleable (and controllable) and more suited to the demands of his insatiable curiosity. In spring 1955 he began work on *Around the World with Orson Welles*, a series of twenty-six half-hour documentaries for the British commercial channel ITV. The programmes used his recent travels as a springboard, but like much of his televised work (the six-episode *Orson Welles' Sketch Book*, for example) they were always dominated by Welles's personality, intellect and physical presence, not to mention the trademark cigar and bow-tie.

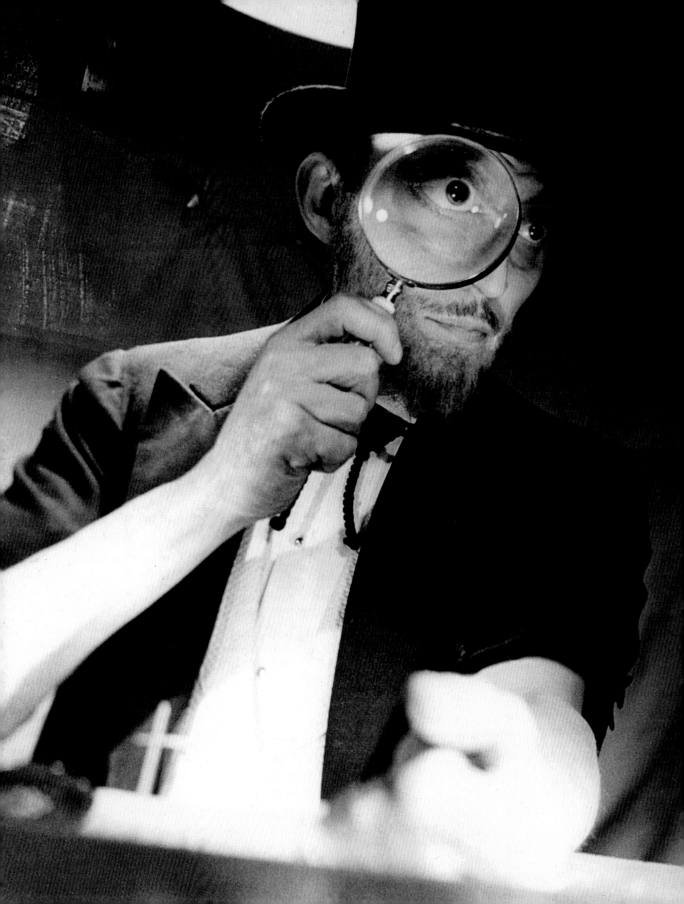

Welles the critic

What do you think of the New Wave French directors so admired by these journals?

I'm longing to see their work! I've missed most of it because I'm afraid it might inhibit my own. When I make a picture, I don't like to refer to other pictures; I like to think I'm inventing everything for the first time. I talk to Cahiers du Cinéma about movies in general because I'm so pleased that they like mine. When they want long highbrow interviews, I haven't the heart to refuse them. But it's a complete act. I'm a fraud; I even talk about 'the art of the cinema'. I wouldn't talk to my friends about the art of the cinema – I'd rather be caught without my pants in the middle of Times Square.

How do you feel about the films of Antonioni?

According to a young American critic, one of the great discoveries of our age is the value of boredom as an artistic subject. If that is so, Antonioni deserves to be counted as a pioneer and founding father. His movies are perfect backgrounds for fashion models. Maybe there aren't backgrounds that good in *Vogue*, but there ought to be. They ought to get Antonioni to design them.

And what about Fellini?

He's as gifted as anyone making pictures today. His limitation – which is also the source of his charm – is that he's fundamentally very provincial. His films are a small-town boy's dream of the big city. His sophistication works because it's the creation of someone who doesn't have it. But he shows dangerous signs of being a superlative artist with little to say.

Ingmar Bergman?

As I suggested a while ago, I share neither his interests nor his obsessions. He's far more foreign to me than the Japanese.

How about contemporary American directors?

Stanley Kubrick and Richard Lester are the only ones that appeal to me – except for the old masters. By which I mean John Ford, John Ford and John Ford. I don't regard Alfred Hitchcock as an American director, though he's worked in Hollywood for all these years. He seems to me tremendously English in the best Edgar Wallace tradition, and no more. There's always something anecdotal about his work; his contrivances remain contrivances no matter how marvellously they're conceived and executed. I don't honestly believe that Hitchcock is a director whose pictures will be of any interest a hundred years from now. With Ford at his best, you feel that the movie has lived and breathed in a real world, even though it may have been written by Mother Machree. With Hitchcock, it's a world of spooks.

This is an extract from Kenneth Tynan, 'Playboy interview: Orson Welles', *Playboy* (March 1967).

Orson Welles and Serge Daney in 1983.

Orson Welles, Janet Leigh and Akim Tamiroff in *Touch of Evil* (1958).

Touch of Evil

Television also offered Welles the chance to work professionally in the United States again. At the beginning of 1956 he made pilots for two TV series, one of which, *The Fountain of Youth*, was eventually broadcast in 1958. However, this work would lead to his return to film as a director: Charlton Heston was contractually bound to make another film for Universal, and producer Albert Zugsmith offered Welles the second lead. But given Heston's increasing popularity (he had just achieved stardom in Cecil B. DeMille's *The Ten Commandments*, 1956), Zugsmith wanted a prestigious name to direct the picture. Welles got the job. *Touch of Evil* (1958), an adaptation of the Whit Masterson novel *Badge of Evil*, deals with the professional and personal confrontation between two policemen: the Mexican Mike Vargas

(Heston), newly married to Susan, and the American Hank Quinlan (Welles). Both men are investigating the assassination of a wealthy American. Quinlan relies solely on his instincts and will stop at nothing, not even the fabrication of evidence. Vargas, by contrast, respects the rules and operates by the book. The conflict between them sucks in the innocent Susan (Janet Leigh) and the Grandi mafia clan, and ultimately leads to a settling of accounts in which Quinlan is betrayed by his trusted colleague.

Welles rewrote the existing screenplay so that Quinlan became as important as Vargas, shifted the action to a Mexican border town and added a series of references to the racial tensions that pervaded the border area. During the shoot, he demonstrated his extraordinary flair for constructing highly complex scenes and overcoming

Janet Leigh and Charlton Heston in *Touch of Evil* (1958).

Marlene Dietrich in
Touch of Evil (1958).

Opposite page: Orson Welles
in *Touch of Evil* (1958).

obstacles as he filmed them: the opening scene, in which a bravura overhead tracking shot combines the killer planting a bomb in the boot of a car and the progress of its unsuspecting passengers towards the border and oblivion, is justly famous. The equally complex scene in which the chief suspect's house is searched — an uninterrupted series of takes completed in a day rather than the three or more days originally envisaged — is also remarkable. However, once again, the editing process led to a crisis with the production company. The 109-minute rough cut Welles sent to Universal, constructed from dozens of compositions and alternating between long continuous sequences and extremely rapid intercutting, had a jagged rhythm designed to continually confound audience expectations. Studio officials were not convinced, imposed 15 minutes of cuts (removing scenes that clarified the film's moral dimension), and added anodyne inserts shot by the little-known director Harry Keller. They also interfered with

the virtuoso opening scene, tacking on credits and music that reduced its tension. The film was eventually released in April 1958.

Despite studio interference, *Touch of Evil* is a masterpiece, a monumental work erected on the foundations of a fairly run-of-the-mill crime novel. And in his portrayal of Quinlan, Welles creates a titanic character: riddled with the disease of absolutism, morally corrupt but gifted with an unerring flair, he embodies the innocence of sin rather than the grandeur of evil. As his friend Tanya (Marlene Dietrich) comments at the end of the film, he may have been 'a lousy cop', but he was 'some kind of a man'. The moral ambiguity at the heart of the story is matched by an aesthetic ambiguity achieved through violent spatial distortions (the preponderant use of wide angles in short focus exaggerates the depth of field, and cameraman Russell Metty creates an extraordinary chiaroscuro effect), and is also emphasized by the totally unpredictable rhythm of the editing.

Don Quixote

The first hard evidence that Welles wanted to adapt Cervantes' *Don Quixote* for the big screen dates back to January 1955. Having completed the shooting of *Mr. Arkadin*, he asked Mischa Auer and Akim Tamiroff to carry out costume tests as Quixote and Panza in the Bois de Boulogne, outside Paris. A concrete opportunity seemed to arise two years later when a television company expressed interest, but nothing came of it. Determined to go ahead with his interpretation of a masterpiece of Spanish literature, Welles used his own money (his fee for playing Will Varner in Martin Ritt's *The Long, Hot Summer*, 1958) to begin filming in Mexico. As Auer was unavailable, Welles cast the Spanish actor Francisco Reiguera as Don Quixote, retaining Tamiroff as Sancho Panza. Welles would introduce the story, recounting some of its episodes to a young American tourist played by Patty McCormack. He assembled a skeleton crew and began shooting in the summer of 1957, intending to confront the knight errant and his squire with the realities of the twentieth century: windmills were replaced by mechanical diggers, and the battle against the Moors took place in a cinema, with Don Quixote charging the shadows on the screen. The film would conclude with a nuclear explosion that wiped out everything except the two immortal heroes. The absence of a preexisting screenplay posed no problem, for as Welles himself recalled, he proceeded 'with a degree of freedom that you wouldn't find in normal productions, because it was done without cutting, without even a narrative thread, without even a synopsis. Every morning, the actors, the crew and I met in front of the hotel, and we took off and invented the film in the street, like Mack Sennett.' (André Bazin and Charles Bitsch, 'Entretien avec Orson Welles', Cahiers du cinéma, 84, June 1958.)

Inevitably, the vagaries of Welles's artistic and economic existence had a considerable impact on the film's fate. Having left America for Europe, he was unable to complete his project; from time to time he would raise enough money to summon his actors and add another stone to the edifice, but it seemed to go on for ever. Despite the major setback caused by Reiguera's death in 1969, he sent Gary Graver to Seville to shoot the Holy Week procession in 1972. Filming effectively stopped that year, when Tamiroff died, although Welles continued to supervise the editing. He worked closely with Renzo and Maurizio Lucidi, then with Peter Parasheles, and finally with Mauro Bonanni, but never managed to produce a final cut. In 1992, Jesús 'Jess' Franco edited the material owned by Oja Kodar. The resulting 115-minute version is frankly disappointing, and does not even contain the scene in which Don Quixote draws his sword and attacks the shadows on the cinema screen.

Orson Welles with Akim Tamiroff as Sancho Panza on the set of *Don Quixote* in 1955.

Francisco Regueira on the set of *Don Quixote* in 1957.

Following pages: Anthony Perkins and Romy Schneider in *The Trial* (1962).

Don Quixote and *The Trial*

Yet again, Welles's hopes of a good working relationship with a major studio had been shattered by the arrogance of its executives. He decided to return to Europe, where, between two acting assignments, he began directing a version of *Don Quixote* set in modern-day Spain, with Francisco Reiguera as Quixote and Akim Tamiroff as Sancho Panza. Filming proceeded intermittently between 1955 and 1972 (the year Tamiroff died), using a variety of formats and sets, but the project was never completed.

However, Welles did complete a relatively faithful adaptation of Franz Kafka's *The Trial*. Undertaken at the suggestion of producer Michael Salkind in 1961, the film was released in December 1962. The story revolves around the employee Josef K. (Anthony Perkins),[16] who is seized by the representatives of a mysterious power and accused of an unidentified crime. At first, the ghostly court before which he appears seems sympathetic, and he rejects the services of a lawyer (a small role that Welles took on after Jackie Gleason turned it down). But K. gradually accepts his victimhood and resigns himself to a death sentence.

Filmed as usual in various parts of Europe — Rome, Milan, Paris, Dubrovnik and Zagreb — *The Trial* benefits from a very strong supporting cast including Jeanne Moreau, Elsa Martinelli (Welles had initially chosen Claudia Cardinale) and Romy Schneider. Some aspects of the adaptation, however, are not wholly convincing. Perhaps the difficulty arises from Welles's continuing

Anthony Perkins in *The Trial* (1962).

determination to pursue his dream of a vision-
ary form of cinema against all odds, a dream that
in this instance is not fully realized despite the
efforts of production designer Jean Mandaroux
and cameraman Edmond Richard. Or perhaps it
arises from the choice of leading actor: Perkins
is the same age as Kafka's protagonist, but his
overly neurotic performance fails to convey the
sense of existential despair that overwhelms Josef
K. in the novel. Perhaps the metaphorical reading
of the secondary characters is a little too facile,
rendering them all (including Welles's lawyer) too

stilted and predictable to be really fascinating. *The
Trial* lacks the unifying power of the other films,
which, although far more difficult to make in
some cases, are more controlled in terms of inspiration. The images that remain in the mind — the
vast 'Piranesian' archives, the oppressive ceilings,
the flight from Titorelli's house along a passage-
way slashed by light and shadow — are no more
than scattered fragments, indications of a crum-
bling universe in which the dream of a possible
harmony is metaphorically denied by the nuclear
mushroom cloud that concludes the film.

Orson Welles and Jeanne Moreau in *Chimes at Midnight* (1966).

Chimes at Midnight

With *Chimes at Midnight* (1966), a much more personal and successful endeavour, Welles revived the
Falstaff character he had already played on stage
(*Five Kings*, 1939, and *Chimes at Midnight*, 1960). In
order to find a producer willing to finance the
project, he agreed to collaborate on an adaptation
of *Treasure Island* by John Hough (1972) and even
directed a few scenes, so great was his desire to
take on the role of Falstaff himself. He worked on
his film from October 1964 to April 1965 and delivered the first cut in December 1965.

Adapted from Shakespeare's *Richard II*, *Henry
IV* (*Parts I* and *II*), *Henry V* and *The Merry Wives of
Windsor*, the action unfolds in England in 1408
and focuses on the relationship between Hal, son
of Henry IV and heir to the throne, and Sir John
Falstaff, an indefatigable teller of tall tales and
enthusiastic imbiber of Spanish wines. Hal's passion for Mistress Quickly's tavern and his drink-
ing sessions with Falstaff, which he prefers to the
Court and the company of his peers, is curtailed by
the Battle of Shrewsbury, where he provokes a duel
with the rebel Hotspur, and by a vision of his father

Orson Welles (bottom, with John Gielgud) on the set of *Chimes at Midnight* (1966).

on his deathbed. He rediscovers his sense of duty as a member of the nobility, and when crowned king denies his past and his friendship with Falstaff. The central theme, the birth of 'modernity', had already been approached in *The Magnificent Ambersons* and is embodied here in the conflict between Hal's two 'fathers' — the cynical, political Henry IV and the vital, spontaneous Falstaff — and by the inevitability of defeat that permeates the history plays: Falstaff's attempts to inculcate the values of humanism in Hal are thwarted because the interests of the kingdom are considered more important. Welles gives us a foretaste of this in the battle scenes (these have an extraordinary visual power: 17 minutes of pure spectacle constructed from 392 different shots), and it will be explicitly expressed by Hal during his coronation as Henry V: 'I know thee not, old man: Fall to thy prayers; How ill white hairs become a fool, and jester!'

Surrounded by a group of perfectly cast actors (Keith Baxter, John Gielgud, Jeanne Moreau, Margaret Rutherford, Norman Rodway, Marina Vlady, Fernando Rey, Alan Webb and the surprising Walter Chiari), Welles creates a melancholy and heartrending character. A new Falstaff emerges here; he cleaves to the 'character' of Welles and reveals a solitude that can no longer be disguised by outrageous behaviour. Despite the numerous liberties Welles takes with the text — the typically Shakespearean notion of the pure and good man who reveals his total inability to relate to the logic of power and must therefore be isolated in order to safeguard the interests of crown and country — he reveals his own tragic and desperate grandeur in this film. Falstaff, defeated, humiliated, rejected, is the most Shakespearean of Wellesian characters precisely because he is a projection of the director himself, achieved through an interpenetration of theatrical text and screenplay that ultimately encompasses lived experience. 'You'll forget me when I'm gone', Falstaff tells Doll; Welles's remark not only emphasizes the tragic nature of his most successful character, but it is also a testament to his own failure as a man and a filmmaker.

The Immortal Story

This theme was clearly very close to Welles's heart, for shortly after completing *Chimes at Midnight* he accepted an offer from the French state broadcasting organization, ORTF, to make another film that

Orson Welles in *The Immortal Story* (1968).

confronted the same issues. No matter what angle we approach it from, *The Immortal Story* (1968) is an absolutely perfect film; it is an 'outright classic', the transparent sum of all the ideas and anxieties that appear in Welles's oeuvre.

Inspired by Isak Dinesen's short story, the film recounts the efforts of Mr Clay, a Macao-based merchant, to re-enact a story he has always believed to be true but that turns out to be the product of vanity and fantasy: a rich old man pays a sailor to sleep with his wife and provide him with an heir. Mr Clay has never married, but he decides to involve the daughter (Jeanne Moreau) of a former associate he has personally ruined and driven to suicide. With

the help of his sinister accountant, Clay hopes to achieve what Kane, Quinlan, Arkadin and Falstaff had pursued in vain: mastery of the destiny of others, a venture that would take him beyond the barrier that hides a world waiting to be created.

But Welles knew only too well that such certainties had gone for ever. Every dream ends in an abrupt awakening. And Clay would certainly be no different: 'He waited until dawn to taste his triumph, but he couldn't resist the conclusion', the narrator informs us. Death has scripted the denouement of a dream that would in any case have been unachievable, for the sailor, genuinely in love with his one-night stand, swears he will never tell anybody about 87 his adventure. The pedantic accountant had understood everything: 'When we add up different numbers, we go from right to left, but if someone decided to go from left to right, what would happen then? The total would be wrong, as well as the account books.' Clay embodies desire and ambition, yet the result he obtains embodies the inevitability of defeat. But perhaps Welles the director had always believed in going from left to right.

F for Fake and *Filming Othello*

After concluding part of his own trajectory as a director in 1968 with *The Immortal Story*, a perfect film that steadily maintains its death-like atmosphere despite various difficulties involved in its genesis (the English version runs for 57 minutes, as opposed to the 50-minute French version), Welles entered a totally new period of his life. The world was gradually acknowledging his stature as an artist. Books and tributes to his life and career proliferated, and on 9 February 1975 the American Film Institute honoured him with its prestigious Life Achievement Award. Universities invited him to speak, and the offers of acting parts, large or small, voice-off or on-screen, poured in. What did not change, however, was his relationship with producers, who continued to deny him the chance to direct despite the constant flow of projects and screenplays he submitted.

During the last twenty years of his life — he died on 10 October 1985 while preparing a project that was meant to start shooting the following day — Welles began work on four more films, two of

Welles and television

At one stage in his career, Welles considered television as a possible creative alternative, for the costs of making a film were rising – at least for him and the kind of shooting he was accustomed to. His first opportunity arose when the British company Associated-Rediffusion (part of the ITV network) commissioned *Around the World with Orson Welles*, a series of twenty-six 30-minute documentaries. The project was devised around Welles himself, exploiting his multi-faceted personality, his love of travel and his insatiable curiosity through a narrative structure based mainly on direct interviews and the presence of more or less famous people to act as guides. Filming came to a halt after the first few episodes, which covered Vienna, the Basque country, London, Paris and bullfighting in Spain. One unfinished episode concerned the notorious Gaston Dominici affair (the murder of an English family near Lurs, in the South of France).

Returning to the United States for an acting assignment in 1956, Welles directed pilots for two television series, but the major national networks were not interested. ABC broadcast *The Fountain of Youth*, featuring Dan Tobin, Joi Lansing and Rick Jason, two years later, but a series with Welles as host and narrator (in the manner of *Alfred Hitchcock Presents*), never came to fruition. Some of his Italian projects were more successful: he directed *Portrait of Gina* (about the actress Gina Lollobrigida), and nine episodes, just under 30 minutes in length and set in Spain, of *Nella terra di Don Chisciotte* (*In the Land of Don Quixote*), co-produced by Italy's public national broadcaster RAI. The list of Welles's unfinished projects is a long one and contains several programmes linked to his work for the theatre, notably *Moby Dick – Rehearsed*, in which he mounts the stage to read extracts from Herman Melville's novel and take questions from the audience, and to his continual wanderings (*Orson's Bag*, in which episodes about London and Vienna were mixed with a 'production' of Shakespeare's *The Merchant of Venice*). He also spent six years (June 1976 to 1982) turning out episodes of *Orson Welles' Magic Show*.

Left: Jeanne Moreau in *The Immortal Story* (1968).

Above: Oja Kodar in 'The Magic Show' in the 1970s.

Following pages: Oja Kodar and Orson Welles in *F for Fake* (1973).

The Other Side of the Wind: a film testament, by Orson Welles

In 1974, Welles worked on The Other Side of the Wind, *in which John Huston would have portrayed a Hollywood director nearing the end of his life. The film was intended to be a kind of testament and a filmic résumé. Welles described its framework and significance.*

This film was imagined as being totally different to all the films that preceded it. In reality it's two films that develop in parallel, and sometimes simultaneously. The first records the final hours of J. J. Hannaford's life. [...]
As eclectic as Hawks (although more poetic), as poetic as Ford (but not so sentimental), Jake Hannaford belongs to their generation, but not to their world. Like Rex Ingram, who is almost forgotten these days, Jake was a vagabond. He shot most of his films as far away from the Californian studios as he could get. [...] The chance to make this film came from a birthday party given by one of his oldest, most faithful friends [...] Zarah Valeska. Zarah had decided that the time had come for the profession's new generations to meet Hannaford and talk to him, but in this respect, and more generally, the party was a fiasco. And the film is the story of a failure. [...] The second film, interwoven with the documentary on Hannaford's last day, is the real film Jake directed, the one he was working on before his death and which is shown to the guests in the private screening room on the ranch. The action of the film is an integral part of the birthday party documentary, but is nevertheless autonomous. It tells a separate story, simply the story of a boy and a girl, and it's conceived as a kind of dream. Jake himself would have rejected the term 'surrealist tale', but we are forced to use it in order to grasp its meaning. After a series of adventures, his hero and heroine come together again in the ruins of what was once a film studio [...] in a strange, unreal world where nothing is true and has never been, and where the very illusion of reality is transformed into dust. Before we arrive at this stage in the film, we have nonetheless understood that Hannaford, as a director and also as a man, is very close to the end of his life. What we don't know is whether or not he wanted this [...] The man had several masks. At the birthday party, the journalists had tried to strip away his mask. Did they succeed? Perhaps the real mystery doesn't concern the nature of his death, but his nature as a man, the definitive truth about the man as an artist, as a maker of masks.

This is an extract from an interview originally published in Spanish in *Dirigido por ... Orson Welles*, 12 (April 1974).

Orson Welles with John Huston and Peter Bogdanovich on the set of *The Other Side of the Wind* in the 1970s.

Opposite page: Orson Welles in *Filming Othello* (1978).

Following pages : Orson Welles in *F for Fake* (1973).

which (*The Deep*, with Oja Kodar, his companion of the later years, and *The Other Side of the Wind*) were never completed. The other two are totally different from anything he had accomplished in the past: *F for Fake* (1973) and *Filming Othello* (1978) are not works of narrative fiction but rather crypto-films, cinematic essays that highlight (for the viewer and all the more so for Welles himself) the feeling of powerlessness he was experiencing. They are by no means minor works or attempts to cash in on his trademark notoriety, as some commentators have suggested, but are rather reflections on his role as an artist, anguished theories on the impossibility of making a film. His face may have been perfect for Champagne commercials,[17] but it inspired less confidence in producers.

Created almost entirely in the cutting room, *F for Fake* combines two investigations: one into the English art forger Elmyr de Hory, a specialist in Post-Impressionist canvases, and the other into Clifford Irving, a journalist who claimed to have met Howard Hughes and to have acquired his autobiography.[18] The film gradually becomes a broader meditation on the art world and its relationship with reality as Welles evokes his own career. He steadily overturns one of the foundations of his own cinematic oeuvre: the authenticity of his own 'registered trademark',

the need to consecrate everything with his own signature. His films bear an official seal — 'My name is Orson Welles' — but when he trains the camera on the facade of Chartres cathedral, the triumphant creation of anonymous artists, a number of illusions crumble, and the film ends with a brilliant but despairing testament to the pointlessness of art, which he seems to believe has lost its purpose, whether in social, historical or cultural terms.

Thus the monument that Welles had erected to himself was destined for destruction at the hands of its creator. After a lifetime's belief in film, he amused himself by demonstrating its lack of foundations, demolishing it in sequence after sequence. He adopted the same approach for *Filming Othello*, a documentary made for German television, in which he explains the importance of montage and recalls the torments engendered by making *Othello*. While useful as a first-hand account of the most tortured film Welles ever directed, it was also the last chance for an artist to put himself on the stage and talk about himself, to attempt to explain his own 'job as a director'. He once defined a film director as 'the man who presides over accidents, but doesn't make them'. Perhaps the confession contains more bitterness and regret than justified pride.

Chronology

1915
6 May. George Orson Welles is born in Kenosha, Wisconsin, to Beatrice Ives Welles and Richard Head Welles.

1918
Theatrical début in *Samson and Delilah* at the Chicago Opera.

1924
10 May. Mother dies at the age of forty-three.

1926
Begins acting in plays at the Todd School for Boys in Woodstock, Illinois.

1930
28 December. Father dies at the age of fifty-eight.

1931
August. Departs for Ireland and is hired as an actor at the Gate Theatre in Dublin.

1933
May. Returns to the United States, directs *Twelfth Night* and films rehearsals from the auditorium with a silent camera. **Summer.** Travels to Morocco and Spain, writes political stories for popular magazines and toys with the idea of becoming a bullfighter. **18 September.** Hired as an actor by Katharine Cornell's touring company.

1934
Publication of *Everybody's Shakespeare*, co-written by Roger Hill. **Summer.** Films *The Hearts of Age*, co-directed by William Vance. **14 November.** Marries Virginia Nicholson.

1935
Works for radio.

1936
Welles and John Houseman are invited to work at the New York headquarters of the Federal Theatre Project. **14 April.** First job as a professional theatre director with a version of *Macbeth* located in Haiti and featuring an all-black cast. **26 September.** Stages a loose adaptation of *An Italian Straw Hat*, a comedy by Eugène Labiche.

1937
8 January. Directs *Doctor Faustus* by Christopher Marlowe. **March.** Plays the lead in the radio series *The Shadow*. **16 June.** Stages the banned *The Cradle Will Rock*, his last directing assignment for the Federal Theatre Project. **11 November.** Stages *Caesar*, the first production of the Mercury Theatre, founded by Welles and John Houseman.

1938
Launch of *The Mercury Theatre on the Air* drama series, broadcast by CBS. **27 March.** Birth of Christopher, daughter of Welles and Virginia Nicholson. **30 October.** Broadcast of H. G. Wells's *The War of the Worlds* causes panic and gains Welles much publicity.

1939
21 August. Signs a contract with RKO to produce, direct, write and act in two feature films. Writes a screenplay for *Heart of Darkness*, adapted from the novella by Joseph Conrad.

1940
1 February. Divorces Virginia Nicholson. **30 July.** Begins filming *Citizen Kane*.

1941
14 April. FBI director J. Edgar Hoover writes a memorandum concerning Welles and his links to 'organizations which are said to be communist in character'. **1 May.** Release of *Citizen Kane*. **25 September.** Norman Foster begins filming the 'My Friend Bonito' episode of *It's All True*. **28 October.** Begins filming *The Magnificent Ambersons*.

1942
February. Begins filming the Rio de Janeiro carnival, then the *jangadeiros* (Brazilian fishermen) episode of *It's All True*. **28 June.** RKO breaks its contract with Mercury Productions. **10 July.** Premiere of *The Magnificent Ambersons*.

1943
12 February. First public screening of *Journey into Fear*. **3 August.** First appearance in *The Mercury Wonder Show*, a magic show staged for US troops. **7 September.** Marries Rita Hayworth. **October.** Publication of his first article for *Free World* magazine. **December.** Welles makes his first appearance in a film he has not directed, Robert Stevenson's *Jane Eyre*.

1944
January. Begins a lecture tour on the threat of fascism. **26 January.** Launch of the radio show *The Orson Welles Almanac* (twenty-six episodes). **1 September.** Gives his first speech in support of Franklin D. Roosevelt's re-election campaign. **17 December.** Birth of Rebecca, daughter of Welles and Rita Hayworth.

1945
22 January. Begins a six-month stint as a daily columnist for the *New York Post*. **13 March.** Launch of the radio show *This Is My Best*. **16 September.** Launch of *Orson Welles Commentaries* for the ABC network.

1946
27 April. The try-out tour for the musical comedy *Around the World* begins in Boston. **2 July.** First public screening of *The Stranger*.

Bernard Herrmann and Orson Welles in the 1930s.

Orson Welles with Joseph Cotten and Dolores Costello on the set of *The Magnificent Ambersons* (1942).

Orson Welles with Duke Ellington in 1943.

Orson Welles with William H. Greene on the set of *It's All True* in 1942.

1947

7 May. Release of King Vidor's *Duel in the Sun*, for which Welles provides the narration. **28 May.** First performance of *Macbeth* in Salt Lake City. **1 December.** Divorces Rita Hayworth.

1948

9 June. *The Lady from Shanghai* is released in the United States. **1 October.** The first version of *Macbeth* is released in the United States.

1950

15 June. Staging in Paris of *The Blessed and the Damned*. **27 December.** The second version of *Macbeth*, shortened and dubbed, is released in the United States.

1951

March. Begins work in London on a radio series, *The Lives of Harry Lime*, in which he takes the leading role.

1952

10 May. First screening of *Othello* at the Cannes Film Festival.

1953

January. Begins work on Steno's *L'uomo, la bestia e la virtù* (*Man, Beast and Virtue*), his first role in a non-English language film. **18 October.** First television appearance, in *King Lear*, directed by Peter Brook.

1954

January. Begins filming *Mr. Arkadin*.

1955

24 April. Launch of the BBC television series *Orson Welles' Sketch Book*. **8 May.** Marries Paola Mori in London. **16 June.** Premiere in London of his play *Moby Dick – Rehearsed*. **11 August.** First UK screening of *Mr. Arkadin*, under the title *Confidential Report*. **October.** Returns to the United States. **13 November.** Birth of Beatrice, daughter of Welles and Paola Mori.

1956

12 January. First performance in New York of *King Lear*.

1958

February. Films *Portrait of Gina* in Italy. **23 April.** First screening of *Touch of Evil* in Los Angeles, California.

1959

August. Resumes filming *Don Quixote* in Italy.

1960

13 February. First performance, in Belfast, of *Chimes at Midnight*. **28 April.** First performance, in London, of Eugène Ionesco's *Rhinoceros*, the last play Welles directs.

1961

April. Begins filming *Nella terra di Don Chisciotte* (*In the Land of Don Quixote*), a series of nine shows for the Italian network RAI.

1962

21 December. First screening, in France, of *The Trial*.

1966

8 May. First screening of *Chimes at Midnight*, at the Cannes Film Festival.

1967

14 April. Welles meets Oja Kodar, who will become his partner until his death. **14 September.** First appearance on an American talk show, *The Dean Martin Show*. **October.** Begins filming the unfinished *Dead Reckoning*, later retitled *The Deep*, in Croatia.

1968

30 September. First release, in France, of *The Immortal Story*. **November.** Begins working with Peter Bogdanovich on a book of conversations (*This is Orson Welles*) that is subsequently published in 1992.

1970

Spring. Settles in Los Angeles. **August.** Begins filming the unfinished *The Other Side of the Wind*.

1974

September. *F for Fake* is shown at the San Sebastián International Film Festival.

1975

9 February. The American Film Institute honours Welles with its Life Achievement Award, of which he is only the third recipient.

1978

10 July. First broadcast, on the German ARD network, of *Filming Othello*.

1985

10 October. Welles dies of a heart attack at his home in Hollywood..

Orson Welles on the set of *The Lady from Shanghai* (1947).

Orson Welles with Romy Schneider on the set of *The Trial* (1962).

Orson Welles with John Gielgud on the set of *Chimes at Midnight* (1966).

Orson Welles in *F for Fake* (1973).

Filmography

ACTOR ONLY

Jane Eyre 1943
by Robert Stevenson

Tomorrow Is Forever 1946
by Irving Pichel

Black Magic 1949
by Gregory Ratoff

Prince of Foxes 1949
by Henry King

The Third Man 1949
by Carol Reed

The Black Rose 1950
by Henry Hathaway

Return to Glennascaul 1951
by Hilton Edwards

Trent's Last Case 1952
by Herbert Wilcox

Man, Beast and Virtue 1953
L'uomo, la bestia e la virtù
by Steno

**Royal Affairs
in Versailles** 1954
*Si Versailles
m'était conté*
by Sacha Guitry

Trouble in the Glen 1954
by Herbert Wilcox

Napoléon 1955
by Sacha Guitry

**Three Cases
of Murder** 1955
by David Eady, George More
O'Ferrall, Wendy Toye

Moby Dick 1956
by John Huston

Man in the Shadow 1957
by Jack Arnold

**The Long, Hot
Summer** 1958
by Martin Ritt

The Roots of Heaven 1958
by John Huston

Compulsion 1959
by Richard Fleischer

Ferry to Hong Kong 1959
by Lewis Gilbert

High Journey 1959
by Peter Baylis

Austerlitz 1960
by Abel Gance

Crack in the Mirror 1960
by Richard Fleischer

David and Goliath 1960
David e Golia
by Ferdinando Baldi, Richard Pottier

La Fayette 1961
by Jean Dréville

King of Kings 1961
by Nicholas Ray

The Tartars 1961
I tartari
by Ferdinando Baldi

'La Ricotta' 1963
by Pier Paolo Pasolini

The V.I.P.s 1963
by Anthony Asquith

The Finest Hours 1964
by Peter Baylis

**Marco
the Magnificent** 1965
*La fabuleuse aventure
de Marco Polo*
by Deny de la Patellière, Raoul Lévy,
Noël Howard

A Man for All Seasons 1966
by Fred Zinnemann

Casino Royale 1966
by Val Guest, Ken Hughes, John
Huston, Joseph McGrath, Robert
Parrish, Richard Talmadge

Is Paris Burning? 1966
Paris brûle-t-il?
by René Clément

**The Sailor
from Gibraltar** 1967
by Tony Richardson

**I'll Never Forget
What's 'Is name** 1967
by Michael Winner

House of Cards 1968
by John Guillermin

The Fight for Rome 1968
Kampf um Rom
by Robert Siodmak

Oedipus the King 1968
by Philip Saville

Tepepa 1968
by Giulio Petroni

**The Battle
of the Neretva** 1969
Bitka na Neretvi
by Veljko Bulajic

The Southern Star 1969
by Sidney Hayers

The Thirteen Chairs 1969
12 + 1
by Nicolas Gessner, Luciano
Lucignani

Catch-22 1970
by Mike Nichols

**Is It Always Right
to Be Right?** 1970
by Lee Mishkin

The Kremlin Letter 1970
by John Huston

**Start the Revolution
Without Me** 1970
by Bud Yorkin

Waterloo 1970
by Sergei Bondarchuk

A Safe Place 1971
by Henry Jaglom

Freedom River 1971
by Sam Weiss

Malpertuis 1971
by Harry Kümel

Ten Days' Wonder 1971
La décade prodigieuse
by Claude Chabrol

**Get to Know
Your Rabbit** 1972
by Brian De Palma

Necromancy 1972
by Bert I. Gordon

Treasure Island 1972
by John Hough

**And Then There
Were None** 1974
by Peter Collinson

**Voyage
of the Damned** 1976
by Stuart Rosenberg

Hot Tomorrows 1977
by Martin Brest

**It Happened
One Christmas** 1977
by Donald Wrye

**Rime of the Ancient
Mariner** 1977
by Larry Jordan

Some Call It Greed 1977
by Tim Forbes

The Greatest Battle 1978
Il grande attacco
by Umberto Lenzi

The Double McGuffin 1979
by Joe Camp

The Muppet Movie 1979
by James Frawley

**The Secret
of Nikola Tesla** 1980
Tajna Nikole Tesle
by Krsto Papic

**History of the
World: Part I** 1981
by Mel Brooks

**The Man Who Saw
Tomorrow** 1981
by Robert Guenette

Butterfly 1982
by Matt Cimber

Hot Money 1983
by Zale Magder

Where Is Parsifal? 1983
by Henri Helman

**The Enchanted
Journey** 1984
by Yakikoto Higuchi

**The Transformers:
The Movie** 1986
by Nelson Shin

Someone to Love 1987
by Henry Jaglom

SHORT FILM

The Hearts of Age 1934
Running time 8 mins. With Orson
Welles, Virginia Nicholson, Paul
Edgerton, William Vance, Charles
O'Neal. A surrealist series of images.
Co-directed by William Vance.

TELEVISION FILMS AND SERIES

**Orson Welles'
Sketch Book** 1955
Running time 6 x 15 mins. With
Orson Welles. A six-episode series.

**Around the World
with Orson Welles** 1955
Running time 7 x 30 mins. With
Orson Welles. A seven-episode documentary series.

**Orson Welles
and People** 1956
Running time 27 mins. With Orson
Welles.

Portrait of Gina 1958
Running time 30 mins. With Vittorio
De Sica, Anna Gruber, Gina Lollo-
brigida, Orson Welles.

The Fountain of Youth 1958
Running time 25 mins. With Orson
Welles, Dan Tobin, Joi Lansing.
Based on the short story 'Youth
from Vienna' by John Collier.

**Nella terra
di Don Chisciotte** 1964
*In the Land
of Don Quixote*
Running time 9 x 30 mins. With
Orson Welles. A nine-episode documentary series about Spain.

**The Orson Welles
Show** 1979
Running time 1h 14. With Orson
Welles, Angie Dickinson, Burt
Reynolds. A television series pilot.

UNFINISHED FEATURE FILMS

It's All True 1941–2
Don Quixote 1955–72
The Deep 1967–9
**The Other Side
of the Wind** 1970–5

FEATURE FILMS

Citizen Kane — 1941

B&W. **Screenplay** Herman J. Mankiewicz, Orson Welles. **Cinematography** Gregg Toland. **Sound** Hugh McDowell, Bailey Fesler. **Production design** Perry Ferguson. **Editing** Robert Wise. **Music** Bernard Herrmann. **Producer** Orson Welles. **Production** Mercury Productions for RKO Radio Pictures. **Running time** 1h 59. With Orson Welles (Charles Foster Kane), Joseph Cotten (Jedediah Leland), Everett Sloane (Bernstein), Dorothy Comingore (Susan Alexander), George Coulouris (Walter Parks Thatcher), Ruth Warrick (Emily Monroe Norton Kane), Ray Collins ('Boss' Jim W. Gettys), William Alland (Jerry Thompson), Agnes Moorehead (Mary Kane).

• A reporter talks to people close to the recently deceased press tycoon Charles Foster Kane in an attempt to discover the meaning of 'Rosebud', Kane's last word.

The Magnificent Ambersons — 1942

B&W. **Co-directors** Fred A. Fleck, Jack Moss. **Screenplay** Orson Welles, Joseph Cotten, Jack Moss, based on the novel by Booth Tarkington. **Cinematography** Stanley Cortez, Harry J. Wild, Nicholas Musuraca. **Sound** Bailey Fesler, Terry Kellum, Earl B. Mounce. **Production design** Mark-Lee Kirk. **Editing** Robert Wise. **Music** Bernard Herrmann. **Producer** Orson Welles. **Production** Mercury Productions for RKO Radio Pictures. **Running time** 1h 28. With Tim Holt (George Amberson Minafer), Anne Baxter (Lucy Morgan), Agnes Moorehead (Fanny Minafer), Joseph Cotten (Eugene Morgan), Dolores Costello (Isabel Amberson Minafer), Ray Collins (Jack Amberson), Richard Bennett (Major Amberson).

• George Amberson stubbornly prevents his widowed mother from marrying Eugene Morgan, the man she loved as a young woman. He thus destroys his own relationship with Eugene's daughter Lucy, and also condemns his family to financial decline.

Journey into Fear — 1943

B&W. **Co-director** Norman Foster. **Screenplay** Joseph Cotten, Orson Welles, based on the novel by Eric Ambler. **Cinematography** Karl Struss. **Sound** Richard Van Hessen. **Production design** Mark-Lee Kirk. **Editing** Mark Robson. **Music** Roy Webb. **Musical direction** Constantin Bakaleinikoff. **Producer** Orson Welles. **Production** Mercury Productions for RKO Radio Pictures. **Running time** 1h 28. With Joseph Cotten (Howard Graham), Dolores del Río (Josette), Everett Sloane (S. Kopeikin), Jack Moss (Peter Banat), Orson Welles (Colonel Haki), Ruth Warrick (Stephanie Graham), Eustace Wyatt (Professor Haller), Edgar Barrier (Kuvetli), Frank Readick (Mathews), Agnes Moorehead (Mrs Mathews).

• An American traveller in Turkey is mistaken for a spy and repeatedly targeted by Nazi agents, but manages to escape their clutches with the aid of Colonel Haki, a local policeman.

The Stranger — 1946

B&W. **Screenplay** John Huston, Anthony Veiller, Orson Welles, based on a story by Victor Trivas, adapted by Trivas and Decla Dunning. **Cinematography** Russell Metty. **Sound** Arthur Johns. **Production design** Perry Ferguson. **Editing** Ernest Nims. **Music** Bronislaw Kaper. **Production** Haig Corporation for International Pictures. **Running time** 1h 33. With Loretta Young (Mary Longstreet Rankin), Edward G. Robinson (Mr. Wilson), Orson Welles (Franz Kindler/Charles Rankin), Billy House (Solomon Potter), Richard Long (Noah Longstreet), Konstantin Shayne (Konrad Meinike).

• Hunting a Nazi war criminal thought to have taken refuge in the United States, investigator Wilson's suspicions fall on a young, married schoolteacher who appears to be a pillar of his small-town community.

The Lady from Shanghai — 1947

B&W. **Screenplay** Orson Welles, based on the novel *If I Die Before I Wake* by Sherwood King. **Cinematography** Charles Lawton, Jr. **Sound** Lodge Cunningham. **Production design** Sturges Carne. **Editing** Viola Lawrence. **Music** Heinz Roemheld. **Production** Columbia Pictures. **Running time** 1h 27. With Orson Welles (Michael O'Hara), Rita Hayworth (Elsa Bannister), Everett Sloane (Arthur Bannister), Glenn Anders (George Grisby), Carl Frank (Galloway), Erskine Sanford (the judge), Ted De Corsia (Sidney Broome).

• A sailor is given a job by a lawyer and falls in love with his employer's wife. Embroiled in a fake suicide that leads to his arrest, he discovers the truth about the woman he thought he loved.

MacBeth — 1948

B&W. **Screenplay** Orson Welles, based on the play by William Shakespeare. **Cinematography** John L. Russell. **Sound** John Stransky, Jr, Garry Harris. **Production design** Fred Ritter. **Editing** Louis Lindsay. **Music** Jacques Ibert. **Producers** Charles K. Feldman, Orson Welles. **Production** Literary Classics Productions and Mercury Productions for Republic Pictures. **Running time** 1h 26 (second version). With Orson Welles (Macbeth), Jeanette Nolan (Lady Macbeth), Dan O'Herlihy (Macduff), Alan Napier (Holy Father), Edgar Barrier (Banquo), Roddy McDowall (Malcolm), Peggy Webber (Lady Macduff), Erskine Sanford (Duncan).

• Urged on by his wife, Macbeth kills his friend Banquo and his family in order to win the throne of Scotland. But the prophecy that he is invincible turns out to be two-edged.

Othello — 1952

B&W. **Screenplay** Orson Welles, based on the play by William Shakespeare. **Cinematography** Anchise Brizzi, G. R. Aldo, George Fanto. **Sound** Umberto Picistrelli. **Production design** Alexandre Trauner. **Editing** Louis Lindsay, Renzo Lucidi, Jean Sacha, John Shepridge, William Morton. **Music** Angelo Francesco Lavagnino. **Production** Mogador Films, Mercury. **Running time** 1h 33. With Orson Welles (Othello), Micheál MacLiammóir (Iago), Suzanne Cloutier (Desdemona), Fay Compton (Emilia), Robert Coote (Roderigo), Michael Laurence (Cassio).

• Employed by the Venetian Republic to command the stronghold of Cyprus, the Moor Othello chooses Cassio as his lieutenant. The jealous Iago persuades Othello that his wife is unfaithful.

Mr. Arkadin / Confidential Report — 1955

B&W. **Screenplay** Orson Welles. **Cinematography** Jean Bourgoin. **Sound** Jacques Lebreton, Terry Cotter. **Production design** Gil Parrondo (Spain), Orson Welles. **Editing** Renzo Lucidi, William Morton. **Music** Paul Misraki. **Production** Filmorsa (Tangiers), Cervantès Films (Madrid). **Running time** 1h 38. With Robert Arden (Guy Van Stratten), Orson Welles (Gregory Arkadin), Paola Mori (Raina Arkadin), Patricia Medina (Mily), Akim Tamiroff (Jakob Zouk), Jack Watling (Bob, Marquis of Rutleigh), Michael Redgrave (Burgomil Trebitsch), Katina Paxinou (Señora Jesus Martinez), Suzanne Flon (Baroness Nagel).

• Millionaire Gregory Arkadin claims to have forgotten his past and hires Van Stratten, a down-at-heel adventurer, to investigate it. In reality, Arkadin wants to eliminate the witnesses to his crimes, and eventually Van Stratten himself.

Touch of Evil — 1958

B&W. **Screenplay** Orson Welles, based on the novel *Badge of Evil* by Whit Masterson. **Cinematography** Russell Metty. **Sound** Leslie I. Carey, Frank Wilkinson. **Production design** Alexander Golitzen, Robert Clatworthy **Editing** Edward Curtiss, Ernest Nims, Aaron Stell, Virgil W. Vogel. **Music** Henry Mancini. **Producer** Albert Zugsmith. **Production** Universal-International. **Running time** 1h 35. With Orson Welles (Hank Quinlan), Charlton Heston (Mike Vargas), Joseph Calleia (Pete Menzies), Janet Leigh (Susan Vargas), Akim Tamiroff (Joe Grandi), Mort Mills (Al Schwartz), Valentin de Vargas (leader of the Grandi nephews), Dennis Weaver (the night manager), Ray Collins (District Attorney Adair), Victor Millan (Manolo Sanchez), Marlene Dietrich (Tanya).

• Mexican detective Mike Vargas investigates a crime on the US–Mexican border and clashes with his unorthodox American counterpart Hank Quinlan, who is prepared to kidnap his wife in order to get rid of him.

The Trial — 1962

B&W. **Screenplay** Orson Welles, based on the novel by Franz Kafka. **Cinematography** Edmond Richard. **Sound** Guy Villette. **Production design** Jean Mandaroux. **Editing** Fritz Muller, Yvonne Martin. **Music** Jean Ledrut. **Producers** Alexander and Michael Salkind. **Production** Paris Europa Productions (Paris), Hisa-Films (Munich), Fi-C-It (Rome). **Running time** 1h 58. With Anthony Perkins (Josef K.), Romy Schneider (Leni), Orson Welles (Albert Hastler), Akim Tamiroff (Rudi Bloch), Max Haufler (Max K., the uncle), Jeanne Moreau (Marika Burstner), Arnoldo Foà (the Inspector), William Chappell (Titorelli), Elsa Martinelli (Hilda), Billy Kearns (Frank, First Assistant Inspector), Jess Hahn (Second Assistant Inspector), Madeleine Robinson (Mrs Grubach), Suzanne Flon, Michael Lonsdale.

100 • Employee Josef K. is summoned

by the emissaries of a mysterious power and accused of an unidentified crime. At first he defies his judges, but he gradually assumes the role of victim and eventually accepts the death sentence.

Chimes at Midnight — 1966

B&W. **Screenplay** Orson Welles, based on the plays by William Shakespeare: *Henry IV* (*Parts I* and *II*), *Richard II*, *Henry V* and *The Merry Wives of Windsor*. **Cinematography** Edmond Richard. **Production design** Orson Welles, José Antonio de la Guerra. **Editing** Fritz Muller, Elena Jaumandreu. **Music** Angelo Francesco Lavagnino. **Production** International Films Española (Madrid), Alpine Productions (Basel) **Running time** 1h 55. With Orson Welles (Sir John Falstaff), Keith Baxter (Henry Monmouth, 'Hal'), John Gielgud (Henry IV), Norman Rodway (Henry Percy, 'Hotspur'), Alan Webb (Justice Robert Shallow), Tony Beckley (Ned Poins), Margaret Rutherford (Mistress Quickly), Jeanne Moreau (Doll Tearsheet), Marina Vlady (Kate Percy), Fernando Rey (Worcester).

• Hal, son of Henry IV, neglects his duties as a member of the nobility and prefers the company of the drunkard Falstaff. After fighting to defend the crown, he renounces his past and his friend.

The Immortal Story — 1968

Screenplay Orson Welles, based on the short story of the same name by Isak Dinesen from her collection *Anecdotes of Destiny*. **Cinematography** Willy Kurant. **Production design** André Piltant. **Editing** Yolande Maurette. **Music** Erik Satie. **Production** Albina Films, ORTF. **Running time** 57 mins. With Roger Coggio (Elishama Levinsky), Jeanne Moreau (Virginie Ducrot), Orson Welles (Mr Clay), Norman Eshley (Povl Velling, the sailor), Fernando Rey (a European).

• A tobacco merchant obsessed by power decides to turn into reality a tale that sailors have handed down from generation to generation: the fable of an impotent husband who

is desperate for an heir and pays a sailor to sleep with his beautiful wife.

F for Fake — 1973

Cinematography Christian Odasso, Gary Graver, Serge Halsdorf, Tomislav Pinter. **Editing** Marie-Sophie Dubus. **Music** Michel Legrand. **Production** Les Films de l'Astrophore (Paris), Saci (Tehran), Janus Film und Fernsehen (Frankfurt). **Running time** 1h 28. With (as themselves) Orson Welles, Elmyr de Hory, Clifford Irving, Oja Kodar, François Reichenbach, Edith Irving, Joseph Cotten, Paul Stewart, Richard Wilson, Richard Drewitt, Laurence Harvey, Nina Van Pallandt, Christian Odasso, David Walsh, Jean-Pierre Aumont.

• Welles uses an investigation into notorious forgers and hoaxers to reflect on the meaning of art, its purpose and its relation to reality.

Filming Othello — 1978

Cinematography Gary Graver. **Editing** Marty Roth. **Production** ARD. **Running time** 1h 23.

• Welles reviews the torturous development of *Othello*, reveals some of the 'secrets' of his working methods and stresses the importance of the editing process.

Selected Bibliography

André Bazin,
Orson Welles: A Critical View,
tr. Jonathan Rosenbaum,
Elm Tree Books, London, 1978.

Chuck Berg and Tom Erskine,
The Encyclopedia of Orson Welles,
Checkmark Books, New York, 2003.

Jean-Pierre Berthomé and François Thomas,
Orson Welles at Work,
Phaidon, London, 2008.

Frank Brady,
Citizen Welles: A Biography of Orson Welles,
Charles Scribner's Sons, New York, 1989.

Robert L. Carringer,
The Making of Citizen Kane,
University of California Press, Berkeley, 1985.

Peter Cowie,
The Cinema of Orson Welles,
Da Capo Press, New York, 1983.

Richard France,
The Theatre of Orson Welles,
Bucknell University Press, Lewisburg, PA, 1977.

Pauline Kael,
The Citizen Kane Book,
Little, Brown, Boston, 1971.

Barbara Leaming,
Orson Welles: A Biography,
Viking Press, New York, 1985.

Joseph McBride,
Orson Welles,
Secker & Warburg, London, 1972.

James Naremore,
The Magic World of Orson Welles,
Southern Methodist University Press, Dallas, 1989.

Robert Stam, Susan Ryan and Catherine Benamou (eds),
'Special Issue on Orson Welles',
Persistence of Vision, 7 (1989).

Orson Welles and Peter Bogdanovich,
This is Orson Welles,
Harper Collins, New York, 1992.

Notes

1. William Vance attended the Todd School for Boys with Welles and also acted in three plays that Welles staged for the school's Summer Festival of Drama (*Trilby*, *Hamlet* and *Tsar Paul*) in 1934. Two years earlier, Vance had directed a somewhat schematic version of *Dr Jekyll and Mr Hyde*.

2. *The Cabinet of Dr. Caligari*, directed by the German filmmaker Robert Wiene, was regarded by French film critic and historian Georges Sadoul as 'the expressionist work *par excellence*', a seminal work of fantastic cinema. The film recounts the control a fairground barker (Werner Krauss) exercises over a sleepwalker (Conrad Veidt), who is forced to commit crimes. However, the entire story may simply be a hallucination experienced by an inmate of an asylum. The distorted perspectives and zigzag streets create an unreal atmosphere, a world in which dream merges with reality in the collective imagination.

3. The prologue was destroyed when Welles's villa in Madrid caught fire in August 1970.

4. From 9 December, when the adaptation of Daphne du Maurier's *Rebecca* was broadcast, the show became known as The Campbell Playhouse.

5. Founded in 1928, RKO had a distinctive, highly innovative policy. The studio did not specialize in any particular genre, but managed to combine highly prestigious productions with more creative and less expensive films. It also distributed films produced by Walt Disney. RKO was responsible for several outstanding pictures, including *King Kong* (Ernest B. Schoedsack and Merian C. Cooper, 1933), *Notorious* (Alfred Hitchcock, 1946) and *Beyond a Reasonable Doubt* (Fritz Lang, 1956). Instead of strengthening the company, its takeover by the tycoon and occasional filmmaker Howard Hughes in 1948 accelerated its decline and it went into liquidation in 1956. George Schaefer, studio head from 1938 to 1942, was instrumental in launching Welles's cinematic career. Schaefer also produced Alfred Hitchcock's *Suspicion* (1941) and gave the go-ahead

for the cycle of horror films, produced by Val Lewton and directed by Jacques Tourneur, that began with *Cat People* (1942).

6. The other four were MGM, Twentieth Century-Fox, Warner Brothers and Paramount. Universal, United Artists and Columbia formed a second tier of less commercially powerful studios.

7. The novella centres on Marlow's journey as he attempts to gather testimony and information on the personality of Kurtz.

8. Herman J. Mankiewicz, an American screenwriter and brother of producer/director Joseph L. Mankiewicz, began his career as a journalist in New York before moving to Hollywood in 1926, where his output included the screenplay for George Cukor's *Dinner at Eight* (1933) and the story for W. S. Van Dyke's *It's a Wonderful World* (1939). As a producer, he worked with the Marx Brothers on *Monkey Business* (Norman Z. McLeod, 1931) and with W. C. Fields on *Million Dollar Legs* (Edward F. Cline, 1932).

9. A prospector, explorer and hunter before becoming a filmmaker, Robert J. Flaherty (1884–1951) made his name with *Nanook of the North* (1922), which depicted the hardships of an Inuit family living on the shores of Hudson Bay. But his relations with Hollywood were strained, and arguments with producers led to the abandonment of *White Shadows in the South Seas* in 1928, and of *Tabu*, co-directed and completed by F. W. Murnau in 1931. Flaherty moved to England, where he worked with the producer/director John Grierson. While in Britain, he made his masterpiece, *Man of Aran* (1934), an account of a fishing family's struggle for survival on the Isle of Aran.

10. Norman Foster (1900–76) came from a theatrical background and made his début as an actor for Paramount in the late 1920s. He turned to directing and moved to Fox, which gave him the chance to direct the *Mr. Moto* series, with Peter Lorre as a Japanese detective. After collaborating with Welles, Foster made three films in Mexico with Ricardo Montalbán before re-

turning to Hollywood, where he had a notable success with *Rachel and the Stranger* (1948).

11. The 'final cut' is the contractually defined right to have the last word on a film's final edit, to decide on the form of the copy that will be released to the public. The final cut is not always a director's prerogative.

12. Originally a sound engineer, Robert Wise (1914–2005) switched to editing and spent much of his early career at RKO, where he worked on Welles's first two films and others such as *The Hunchback of Notre Dame* (William Dieterle, 1939) and *My Favourite Wife* (Garson Kanin, 1940). Wise made his directorial début with the Val Lewton-produced *The Curse of the Cat People* (1944) and also made *Mademoiselle Fifi* (1944) and *The Body Snatcher* (1945) with Lewton. He went on to demonstrate a thoroughly professional grasp of genre material, including the boxing drama *The Set-Up* (1949), the melodrama *I Want to Live!* (1958), the thriller *Odds Against Tomorrow* (1959), the musical *West Side Story* (1961) and the science-fiction epic *Star Trek: The Motion Picture* (1979).

13. Republic Pictures, a specialist in B films, was founded by Herbert J. Yates in 1935. Yates acquired and amalgamated three small companies on the verge of bankruptcy and began churning out serials and westerns starring Gene Autry, John Wayne and Roy Rogers. But the studio also produced more ambitious films (in artistic if not in budgetary terms) such as Raoul Walsh's *Dark Command* (1940), Allan Dwan's *Sands of Iwo Jima* (1949), John Ford's *Rio Grande* (1950) and *The Quiet Man* (1952), and Nicholas Ray's *Johnny Guitar* (1954). In 1951, Republic became the first studio to sell its films to television. In 1958, it ceased film production in order to concentrate exclusively on television.

14. Among the many actors who were supposed to join the shoot but never materialized were Michel Simon, Alida Valli, Ingrid Bergman and Marlene Dietrich.

15. Arkadin entertains his guests with the following tale: 'Now I'm going to tell you about a scorpion.

This scorpion wanted to cross a river. So he asked a frog to carry him. No, said the frog, no thank you. If I let you on my back you may sting me, and the sting of a scorpion is death. Now where, asked the scorpion, is the logic of that? (Scorpions always try to be logical.) If I sting you, you will die and I will drown. So the frog was convinced and allowed the scorpion on his back. But just in the middle of the river he felt a terrible pain and realized that after all the scorpion had stung him. Logic, cried the dying frog as he started under, bearing the scorpion down with him, there is no logic in this! I know, said the scorpion, but I can't help it. It's my character.'

16. In Robert Mulligan's *Fear Strikes Out* (1957), Perkins portrayed a fragile, tormented young man, a role that would subsequently lead to typecasting, most notably as the schizophrenic murderer in Alfred Hitchcock's *Psycho* (1960). Despite opportunities to vary his repertoire in Anatole Litvak's *Goodbye Again* (1961) and Welles's *The Trial* (1962), he was soon forced to revert to type, playing mentally disturbed and even psychopathic characters. He appeared in two remakes of Hitchcock's masterpiece, the second of which, *Psycho III* (1986), marked his début as a director.

17. The upper half of the publicity page for Veuve Clicquot Champagne was filled by a silhouette of Welles. Readers were invited to identify him using the text below, which offered clues in the form of highlights from his career, beginning with 'The War of the Worlds' radio broadcast.

18. The tyrannical billionaire Howard Hughes (1905–1976) was a major character in twentieth-century American life and had numerous dealings with film as a director and producer. In 1948 he took control of RKO and ran it until 1955, backing films such as John Farrow's *Where Danger Lives* (1950) and Josef von Sternberg's *Macao* (1952). Martin Scorsese depicted his early life in *The Aviator* (2004). Besides *F for Fake*, the last twenty years of his life, spent in isolation, were examined in *Melvin and Howard* (Jonathan Demme, 1980) and *The Hoax* (Lasse Hallström, 2006).

Sources

Collection Cahiers du cinéma: inside front cover–p.1, pp.2, 4–5, 6, 10–1, 12, 14, 16, 20, 21, 22–3, 24, 26–7, 28, 29, 30–1, 32, 33, 36–7, 38, 39, 40–1, 42, 44–5, 46, 47, 50–1, 52–3, 54–5, 57, 58–9, 61, 62, 63, 64, 65, 66, 68, 69, 70–1, 72, 73, 74–5, 76, 77, 80–1, 82, 84–5, 87, 88–9, 89, 90–1, 93, 94–5, 97 (1st col.), 103, 106.
Collection Cahiers du cinéma/Archives

Finnegan's Enguerrand: p.17.
Collection Cahiers du cinéma/D. Rabourdin: pp.43, 104–inside back cover.
Collection Cahiers du cinéma/Vincent Pinel: pp.18–19, 56, 60.
Collection CAT'S: cover, pp.34–5, 48–9.
Collection Cinémathèque française: pp.13, 78,79, 83, 86, 96 (3rd col.).
Collection Gary Graver: p.92.

Collection Jean-Pierre Berthomé et François Thomas: p.9.

Credits

© All rights reserved: pp.2, 6, 7, 8, 9, 12, 13, 17, 22–3, 36–7, 38, 57, 64 (2nd col.), 72, 84–5, 89, 92, 93, 94–5, 97 (2nd and 4th col.), 103.
© Arco Film/Cinerez/Société cinémato-graphique Lyre: p.65.
© CBS: pp.10–1, 42, 43.
© Caren Roberts-Frenzel: p.25.
© Columbia: inside front cover–p.1, pp.44–5, 46, 47, 48–9, 50–1, 52–3, 97 (1st col.), 106.
© Didier Deleskiewicz: pp.4–5.

© Films Marceau/Mercury Productions/The Orson Welles Estate: pp. 60, 61, 62, 63.
© Focus Film Entertainment: p.16.
© INA: pp.87, 88–9.
© Les films de l'Astrophore: pp.90–1.
© London Film Production/British Lion Film Corporation: p.64 (1st col.).
© Mercury Productions/Sevilla: pp.66, 68, 69, 70–1.
© Nicolas Tikhomiroff/Magnum Photos: pp.83, 86.
© Oja Kodar: pp.78, 79.

© Paris Europa Films: pp.80–1, 82.
© Paul Carpentier: p.96 (3rd col.).
© Republic Pictures: pp. 54–5, 56, 58–9.
© RKO: pp.14, 18–9, 20, 21, 24, 26–7, 28, 29, 30–1, 32, 33, 34–5, 39, 40–1, 104–inside back cover.
© Universal: pp.73, 74–5, 76, 77, 100 (1st col. top).
© Universal Pictures: cover.

All reasonable efforts have been made to trace the copyright holders of the photographs used in this book. We apologize to anyone that we were unable to reach.

Opposite page: Orson Welles in the 1960s.
Cover: Orson Welles in Jack Arnold's *Man in the Shadow* (1957).
Inside front cover: Orson Welles and Rita Hayworth in *The Lady from Shanghai* (1947).
Inside back cover: Everett Sloane, Orson Welles and Joseph Cotten in *Citizen Kane* (1941).

Cahiers du cinéma Sarl
65, rue Montmartre
75002 Paris

www.cahiersducinema.com

Revised edition © 2011 Cahiers du cinéma Sarl
First published in French as *Orson Welles* © 2007 Cahiers du cinéma Sarl

ISBN 978 2 8664 2701 6

Series conceived by Claudine Paquot
Concept designed by Werner Jeker/Les Ateliers du Nord
Designed by Pascaline Richir
Translated by Roger Leverdier
Printed in China